Book # 2
Darryl Weiman

Fundamental Issues in Health Care Law

Facts for the Health Care Professional

A Lecture Series

Darryl S. Weiman, M.D., J.D.
Professor, Cardiothoracic Surgery
University of Tennessee Health Science Center
Chief, Surgical Service, VAMC Memphis
Author, Medical Malpractice, A Physician's Guide

www.MedicalMalpracticeAndTheLaw.com

Creative Team Publishing

Creative Team Publishing
San Diego

Disclaimer: The opinions and conclusion expressed in this book are strictly those of the author and do not necessarily represent or express the policies and procedures of the U.S. Department of Veterans Affairs or The University of Tennessee Health Science Center

ISBN: 978-0-9903398-2-3

PUBLISHED BY CREATIVE TEAM PUBLISHING
www.CreativeTeamPublishing.com
San Diego

Printed in the United States of America

The Lecture Series and The Author

Dr. Darryl S Weiman is well-qualified to present this lecture series. The series, composed of 13 talks, addresses essential topics in Health Care Law and presents the facts that a health care professional must know.

Darryl S. Weiman, M.D., J.D. is a Fellow of the American College of Surgeons and a member of the American Association of Thoracic Surgeons. He is a graduate of Northwestern University where he majored in Biomedical Engineering. Dr. Weiman did his medical school training at Saint Louis University.

After medical school, he did his General Surgery residency at the University of Chicago and his Cardiothoracic residency at Long Island Jewish Hospital. While maintaining an active practice in cardiothoracic surgery at the University of Tennessee Health Science Center, Dr. Weiman obtained a legal education at the Cecil C. Humphreys School of Law at the University of Memphis. He passed the Bar Exam for the State of Tennessee.

Dr. Weiman continues to be a Professor of Surgery at the University of Tennessee Health Science Center and is the Chief of Surgery at the VA Medical Center in Memphis.

Although he does not practice law, he does research on health care issues and speaks and publishes on some of these topics. Dr. Weiman has presented as a visiting professor on numerous occasions.

You are encouraged to write notes as these lectures are presented. Use this book as a study guide as well as an information-rich collection of useful facts.

Additional information on the lecture series and other products and serves are available on Dr. Weiman's website:

www.MedicalMalpracticeAndTheLaw.com

Fundamental Issues in Health Care Law

Facts for the Health Care Professional

A Lecture Series

Darryl S. Weiman, M.D., J.D.

www.MedicalMalpracticeAndTheLaw.com

Dedication

I dedicate *Fundamental Issues in Health Care Law—Facts for the Health Care Professional: A Lecture Series* to the many surgeons, physicians, and lawyers who have given me the knowledge base to do what I do to help take care of my patients.

Table of Contents

*****

Remember: with knowledge comes power.
I designed this lecture series to help the health care professional better cope with the legal processes they will confront when the law and medicine meet.

Talk #1: Introduction to Law

The sources of law in the United States are written constitutions, either Federal or state, statutes, rules of administrative bodies, and the common law.

Constitutions make up the supreme laws of the land but they are prone to ambiguity. Many legal battles are fought to determine what the constitutions mean on a particular issue.

Statutes are written laws which come from legislative bodies, again Federal or state. Oftentimes, the wording in the statute is ambiguous. It's then up to the judges involved in cases or controversies to interpret what the law actually is. In interpreting the meaning of the written laws, there are certain "rules of construction" that the judges use.[1] First, they read the words and then use the word's *common* meaning to derive an understanding of what the legislators were trying to convey. If the common meaning of the words fails to clarify the situation, many judges will then go to the record of the legislative history so as to better understand what the law makers were trying to do.

Pragmatism is when some judges weigh the consequences of one interpretation over another. In regard to rules, Judge Richard A. Posner said, "A frequent criticism of the canons of construction is that for every canon one might bring to bear on a point there is an equal and opposite canon. This is an exaggeration; but what is true is that there is a canon to support every possible result."[2]

Many appellate court decisions come from a divided bench. When a decision is not unanimous, judges on the losing side may find it necessary to write minority opinions which can then be used by judges to later overturn the present, winning opinion. The vast majority of the time spent in law school is spent reading appellate decisions to learn how judges derive what the law is. Law students look at the written statutes, but that is only a small part of the learning process.

After a law has been passed by the legislative body, it must be finalized by a signature of the Executive; for laws passed by the United States Congress, the President would sign off, and for laws passed by the State's legislative bodies, the governors would sign off.

Administrative bodies have a role after a law has been passed and signed by the Executive. The administrative body usually has been given the power by the legislature to do what it has to do to enforce the law. Examples of administrative bodies that have written extensive rules to enforce the law are the Center for Medicare and Medicaid, the Food and Drug Administration, the Environmental

Protection Agency, the Federal Trade Commission, and the Internal Revenue Service.

Lastly, Common Law is a distinct body of law that is not written by the legislative bodies or administrative agencies. It's based on previous judicial decisions.

The common law is based on what the appellate judges deem the law to be. The *holdings* of the appellate court are the law. Since the judges don't have the time to research all of the issues being brought to them, they are dependent on the attorneys from both sides of the issue to do the legal research and present the arguments in the form of a *brief.* A brief, according to Black's Law Dictionary, is "[a] written statement setting out the legal contentions of a party in litigation, especially on appeal; a document prepared by counsel as the basis for arguing a case, consisting of legal and factual arguments and the authorities in support of them."[3]

Note: a brief is often over a hundred pages in length—although there are some courts that have rules on how long a brief can be.

It's not just the opposing attorneys who write briefs; others who have a stake in the decision often provide their own briefs to the judges as "Friends of the Court."

Cases that make it to the Supreme Court often have numerous "Friends of the Court" briefs as the decision may have national import and both sides will strive mightily to get their legal arguments in front of the judges, or the clerks of the judges, in hopes that they may convince a critical swing vote in their favor.[4]

Often appellate judges have their own idea as to how the litigation should be decided and they will pick and choose arguments from the various briefs that support their opinion. If you ever have the opportunity to read an appellate court opinion, you'll understand how difficult it would be if the judges had to do their own legal research for each and every case they have to decide. The fact that many of their opinions are lengthy and well cited with previous legal decisions makes it clear that the work is probably being done by others such as lawyers involved in the case and friends of the court. The judges, usually in the form of their clerks who have been asked to do the initial writing of the opinion, will use these documents as the basis for their written opinions.

No judge can be expected to know all of the pertinent legal precedents or the statutes pertaining to all of the cases coming before them and that's why it's important to hire an attorney who can present strong written arguments that the judges can then use to support their own written opinions.

There are lawyers who make their livings in substantial part by writing appellate briefs. They are taught to write briefs in law school and it usually doesn't matter which side they may think is right. Law students are trained to vigorously argue for the side of their client. Sometimes lawyers who have been nominated to a federal judgeship may be asked to explain some of their written opinions to the legislative body who will be responsible for confirming them to the position. If their opinion is controversial, the lawyer can try to dodge the issue by explaining that they were only writing for the side of their client and their own opinions had nothing to do with the writing.

"Where the common law governs, the judge, in what is now the forgotten past, decided the case in accordance with morality and custom and later judges followed his decision. They did so by construing the words of his judgment. They looked for the reason which made him decide the case the way he did. [I]t was the principle of the case, not the words, which went into the common law." Patrick Devlin, The Judge 177(1979).[5]

This is a good place to discuss the doctrine of *stare decisis*—to abide by decided cases. This doctrine was instituted to ensure stability to the legal system. The parties to a conflict could surmise the consequences of their actions based on decisions in their jurisdiction that have been made under similar circumstances.

Notice the words *in their jurisdictions.* Stare decisis means that lower courts need to abide by the decisions of the appellate courts in their jurisdiction. These appellate courts would be what Al Gore refers to as "controlling legal authority." Stare decisis works in a downward direction, not horizontally. This means that one state does not need to abide by the decisions of another state, and one federal circuit does not need to follow the decisions of another federal circuit. However, everyone must follow the decisions of the United States Supreme Court.

The bottom line of the doctrine is that courts will usually abide by earlier judicial decisions when the same or similar points arise again in litigation. The courts will follow precedent and not make new law, unless they decide to change the law, which they have the power to do.

Not surprisingly, there is a hierarchy of the law. The Constitution of the United States is the supreme law of the land. Next comes federal laws and federal treaties. State constitutions are next followed by state laws and then local laws.

The United States has three branches of government: the legislative branch is *bicameral;* it has a House of Representatives and a Senate. The executive branch is run by an elected president and the last branch is the judicial branch. It may be a simplification, but the legislative branch writes the laws, the executive branch enforces the laws, and the judicial branch says what the law is.

While the Constitution of the United States is the supreme law, it is full of ambiguities and the language reflects the language of the 1700s which may make it difficult to understand for the modern reader. So which branch has the final authority as to the meaning of the Constitution? Good question. The Constitution itself does not say who will be the final arbiter.

In 1803, John Marshall, the Chief Justice of the Supreme Court, weighed in on this critical issue in the case of *Marbury v. Madison.*[6] This decision is one of the most important in the history of the United States and is discussed below as to better understand how the judicial system works in our country.

The conflict arose when William Marbury was appointed to be a Justice of the Peace for the District of Columbia. The appointment was given by then President John Adams shortly before he was to leave office. Unfortunately for Marbury, the commission wasn't delivered as was required before Adams left office. The Secretary of State who was responsible for delivering the commission was John Marshall, the same John Marshall who was appointed by Adams to take over as the Chief Justice.

By today's standards, any Supreme Court justice who was involved with a case or controversy that eventually makes its way to the Supreme Court would likely recuse themselves from hearing the case. These standards were not in place at that time as there was no mention of Marshall even considering recusal. This has huge historical significance as the decision is arguably the most important decision ever made by the Supreme Court.

When Thomas Jefferson assumed the office of President, he didn't want the judges appointed by Adams to be seated. Apparently, Adams and Jefferson were not friends not unlike the enmity we see in our two political parties today. Jefferson directed his Secretary of State, James Madison, to withhold the commissions of Marbury and some other judges who had recently been appointed by Adams so as to effectively block the judges from assuming their duties.

Marbury then petitioned the United States Supreme Court to issue a writ of *mandamus*[7] to force Madison to deliver the commission.

The powers of the Supreme Court are delineated under Article 3 of the Constitution, and the power to issue a writ of mandamus is not one of those powers. However, the

Congress had given the Supreme Court the power to issue the writs under Section 13 of the Judiciary Act of 1789. So here was a situation where the Congress had actually written laws which would expand the powers of the Supreme Court. Could they do that? Obviously, they thought they could.

About that time, Jefferson was making it very clear that if the writ of mandamus was delivered to Madison, he would direct Madison to ignore the writ. As far as Jefferson was concerned, the commissions, having not been delivered on time, were void.

A constitutional crisis was brewing. Marshall recognized the difficult position he was in. Should he issue the writ knowing that he did not have the power to enforce it or should he just save face by not issuing the writ and letting Jefferson have his way? Either course of action would be looked upon as a significant weakening of the Supreme Court's power.

History has judged Marshall's course of action to be a judicial stroke of genius. Many legal scholars believe that *Marbury v. Madison* is the most important decision ever made by the Supreme Court. It's even more remarkable because, by today's standards, Marshal would have had to recuse himself as he was one of the original players in the conflict.

By a unanimous 4-0 decision, the Court noted that (1) Marbury had a right to his commission; (2) by not delivering the commission, the government had violated a vested legal right of Marbury; but (3) the Court did not have the power vested in the Constitution to issue writs of mandamus.

Marbury had argued that the Constitutional powers granted to the Court were only intended to be the floor of the original jurisdiction and that Congress could add to those powers if it so chose. Marshall disagreed. The Court held that the Congress did not have the authority to add more powers to the Court and, of course, this meant that the Constitution and the Judiciary Act of 1789 were in conflict.

Marshall dealt with the conflict by noting that the Constitution must take precedence and the courts must follow the Constitution when Acts of Congress conflicted. This set up the principle of Judicial Review whereby the Court would decide what law applies when two laws conflict. It also gave the Supreme Court the power to decide on the constitutionality of the laws passed by the Congress. Marshall's reasoning included the judge's oath to uphold the Constitution and the Supremacy Clause of the Constitution which lists the Constitution to be above all the "laws of the United States."

"So, if a law [e.g., a statute or treaty] be in opposition to the Constitution, if both the law and the Constitution apply to a particular case, so that the Court must either decide that case conformably to the law, disregarding the Constitution, or conformably to the Constitution, disregarding the law, the Court must determine which of these conflicting rules govern the case. This is of the very essence of judicial duty. The Courts are to regard the Constitution, as the Constitution is superior to any ordinary act of the

Legislature, the Constitution, and not such ordinary act, must govern the case to which they both apply."[8]

Although Jefferson disagreed with Marshall's reasoning, he let it go because he essentially got what he wanted. Marbury and the others involved in the action never became justices or judges. Their remedy would have involved bringing suit against the United States in a lower Federal court and letting the process run its course. The litigation could have run on for years. Since Marbury never became a justice, one only assumes that he dropped the case. This case shows that the angst involved with judicial appointments dates all the way back to Thomas Jefferson's term.

Jefferson had this to say about the decision, ". . . if this view of judicial power became accepted, it would be 'placing us under the despotism of an oligarchy.'" But he didn't fight the decision. By giving up the fight, *stare decisis* kicked in and from that point on, it has been the Court that acquired final say as to what the Constitution means, i.e., what the law is. In effect, the Court now had the power to declare acts of Congress and other law making bodies, unconstitutional. By grabbing this power, the Supreme Court became an important cog in the *checks and balances* envisioned by the framers of the Constitution.

There are many today who believe that Jefferson was right. The Court, they argue, acts like an oligarchy and the uproar created by the Court's decision in *Bush v. Gore*[9]—which essentially ended the recount on the 2000 Presidential election--is used to bear that belief out. The fact that further counting confirmed that Bush would have won the election anyway does nothing to change the stance that the Court stepped in when it had no business doing so.

Here is a word of caution. I previously mentioned that the decisions made at the appellate court level are considered to be *the law*. This law is what is found in the *holding* of the court. Everything else that is written in the court's opinion that is dealing with associated issues, but is not in the *holding* is called *dictum* the plural of which is *dicta.*[10] Although the *dicta* can give you an idea about how the court would rule in the future if these issues were to come up as the main cause of action, they do not have the force of law. *Dicta* are opinions and they are held to be authoritative because they are being given by the judges, but they generally are not essential to the decision of the case; therefore they are not part of the law.

Be careful: just because you find wording that seems to be supportive of your case, you cannot cite it as legal precedent unless it is the holding. It's your lawyer's job to sort these things out as it is a major skill that they hopefully will have attained in law school.

By giving up the powers granted in the Judiciary Act of 1789, Marshall gained a much greater power for the Supreme Court. It was at that time that the Supreme Court finally became a co-equal partner in the government of the United States.

As for final decisions, the holdings of the Supreme Court of the United States take precedence over all other courts. It is said that the Supreme Court is not last because it is right, it is right because it is last.

Marbury v. Madison

- Jefferson gets what he wants so he does not dispute the Court's holding, but…
- By doing so, the precedent is set that the Supreme Court will have final say on what the Constitution means.
- This holds true even to this day.

Talk #1: Introduction to Law

Review, Recall, and Action

Citations

[1] Rule of construction—also known as a canon of construction; these are "rules used in construing legal instruments, esp. contracts and statutes." Black's Law Dictionary, Seventh Edition.
[2] Richard A. Posner, The Federal Courts: Crisis and Reform 276, (1985). In Black's Law Dictionary, Seventh Edition.
[3] Black's Law Dictionary, Seventh Edition.
[4] For example, *Roe v. Wade,* or *Bush v. Gore.*
[5] Id.
[6] *Marbury v. Madison,* 5 U.S. (1 Cranch) 137 (1803).
[7] "A writ issued by a superior court to compel a lower court or a government officer to perform mandatory or purely ministerial duties correctly. Black's Law Dictionary.
[8] 5 U.S. (1 Cranch) at 177-78.
[9] *Bush v. Gore.*
[10] Dictum; a statement of opinion or belief held to be authoritative because of the dignity of the person making it. Black's Law Dictionary, Seventh edition, Bryan Garner, editor-in-chief.

Talk #2:
Health Courts

America's current system of dealing with the tort of medical malpractice is out of control. Juries often fail in reaching reasonable awards and they have difficulties in differentiating victims of malpractice from those who have suffered from an unavoidable outcome.

Only two percent of patients injured by negligent care in a hospital ever file a malpractice claim (NEJM vol. 324, 1991 (370-6). The elderly and the poor are even less likely to sue (Medical Error: What do we know? What do we do? Jossey-Bass, 2002). Going to court for a trial has been likened to rolling dice; you can never be sure what a jury will decide.

Sean White of Kingsport, Tennessee, claims that "lawyers have brainwashed the public with TV advertisements suggesting that anybody who ever had a bad outcome is a victim of medical malpractice, because there is no way that bad things could ever happen otherwise."

In Tennessee, heart surgeons get sued for malpractice on the average of once every three years. One suit, dating back to an operation in 1996, finally went to trial with an eventual defense verdict in 2013. In this case, the original judge died and a second recused herself since she knew one of the defendants. So much for the concept of a speedy trial as a Constitutional right.

In an effort to circumvent some of the problems inherent with the present tort system, alternative court systems are being considered to make the process quicker and the monetary awards more consistent.

With the current medical malpractice system, most patients harmed by medical malpractice are not compensated. Physicians, practicing defensive medicine, cause more health care dollars to be spent by ordering extra tests and procedures whose purpose is to fend off potential malpractice allegations as opposed to being clinically indicated for their patients.

The current malpractice adjudication system is unpredictable, emotionally draining, and inefficient; cases can drag on for ten years or more. The system relies on juries to reach a verdict based on the law and the facts of the particular case. These juries cannot set precedent. As a result, jury verdicts may be inconsistent with similar cases. There is a belief that proper standards of care should be for the judges to decide, not juries, but that is not how the present system works.

Because of the noted shortcomings of the present system, there have been proposals in the United States Congress, both in the House and Senate, to allocate money to the states to experiment with "Health Courts" and other alternatives to the present system of litigation, for resolving medical malpractice claims.

Under the Affordable Care Act (ACA), there is money set aside for the States to set up Health Courts. These Health Courts will allow for special judges who will be empowered to make rulings on standards of care as a matter of law. Medical experts will be hired by the Courts to opine on the issues of standard of care, causation, and damages. Under the present system, these experts are hired by the parties; this leads to a "battle of the experts" as to how these issues should be resolved.

The proposed Health Court system will have a liberalized standard for negligence; a mistake or medical treatment falling outside a range of good practice will be compensable. The plaintiff will no longer have the burden of persuasion to show personal fault on the part of the defendant.

The Health Courts are designed to expedite proceedings and improve patient access to the system. There will be limits on non-economic damages which will be based on the severity of injury. Damages will be set by an independent commission created by the Congress of the United States.

The Health Courts will be allowed to adjudicate claims against health plans as to coverage decisions. This means the courts will have more jurisdiction than just for medical negligence cases. There will be public reporting of all cases settled or adjudicated. This would constitute a means of setting precedent for other courts dealing with similar fact patterns.

What about the constitutional right to a jury trial? The Seventh Amendment states in part, "[i]n Suits at common law, where the value in controversy shall exceed twenty dollars, the right of trial by jury shall be preserved..." The U.S. Constitution does not prohibit Congress or the States from creating new compensation rights or eliminating claims that were recognized by common law so long as any changes were part of a comprehensive administrative scheme that provides benefits for the claimant. *New York Central Railroad v. White* 243 U.S. 188, 200 (1917).

The benefits of this proposed Health Court system would be (1) quicker and more reliable justice, (2) improved patient safety, (3) lower overall costs, (4) a process to allow for a more trusting and open relationship with physicians and other health care providers, and (5) a liberalized compensation scheme to cover avoidable injuries without the requirement of proving negligence. (Bulletin of the American College of Surgeons, May 2006)

The Health Court system would require an initial claim to be reviewed by a Health Court review board. If the board concludes that the injury was clearly due to malpractice, the claim would be paid according to a published schedule of benefits. These claims would result in expedited payments since they would fit the definition of an Accelerated Compensation Event (ACE). Examples of an ACE would be giving a drug to a patient who is known to be allergic to the drug, amputating or otherwise operating on the wrong extremity, or unintentionally leaving a foreign body inside a patient who had been operated on.

If the board is certain that the claim was not due to malpractice or the injury was too small to justify an award, they can dismiss the case.

For cases that are not clear, a Health Court trial will be the next step in the process. These trials will be presided over by "specially qualified judges" with a background in science or medicine. The models being discussed do not require the judge to have any legal training but this may change during the legislative debates or administrative clarifications.

The Progressive Policy Institute has a plan that would have the judges appointed by the governors. The judges would have to have a background in science and/or medicine. It is uncertain as to how much science (hard or social) would be required and how much medicine. It is also not clear if the judge would need to be a medical doctor; would nurses and PhD's be allowed?

The Health Courts will have the power to hire their own experts to help explain the issues of standard of care and causation. Lawyers would be allowed to be present during the proceedings but there would be no juries.

The legal standards would be liberalized to make it easier for the plaintiff to get some compensation.

The expert witnesses would help the judges make binding determinations as to standards of care, causation, compensation, and related issues such as comparative fault. The experts would be considered neutral to the outcome of the case.

There will be a new legal standard as to what constitutes an injury. An "injury" will be the result of a mistake that should have been prevented. An injury would not occur if optimal care had been given. This is known as the "avoidability" standard; it is more liberal than negligence but not as pure as the "no fault" standard. Plaintiff will no longer need to prove that the defendant breached the standard of care by acting negligently. They will only need to prove that optimal care was not given, a much easier standard to prove.

If liability is found in the Health Court system, damages would be set by a schedule of benefits. This schedule would cover both economic and non-economic damages. This schedule would be developed through a "consensus" process involving research into similar benefit schedules in the U.S. and abroad.

Non-economic damages would be listed in a tiered system based on a severity of injury. This damage schedule would be adjusted annually on the federal level and then used by the health courts in the states.

There are other compensation models for people who are injured but they are all "no fault" models. These previously created models are based on federally created public rights. They provide compensation to injured persons regardless if negligence is involved. There is no deterrence function with these models since there is no defendant at risk of liability.

Worker's Compensation, Vaccine Injury Compensation, The Price-Anderson Act of 1957, and the Air Transportation

Safety and System Stabilization Act of 2001 are examples of compensation systems previously set up for injured parties. All are "no fault" and all have automatic compensation for the victims.

The Health Court system seems like a reasonable idea to bring more fairness to compensating patients who have been injured by health care providers. Physicians like it; insurance companies like it; Republicans like it; the Institute of Medicine likes it.

Lawyers hate it! In fact, the American Bar Association (ABA) adopted a resolution opposing the creation of Health Courts in 2006. The resolution stated that the ABA has "a strong history of firmly supporting the integrity of the jury system, the independence of the judiciary and the right of consumers to receive full compensation for their injuries, without any arbitrary caps on damages."[11]

The ABA points out that the Health Courts would take away an injured patient's right to a jury trial without providing a system that offers equal or better protection. The proposed payout schedule would, in fact, be a de facto cap on non-economic injury claims; some of these caps have already been found to be unconstitutional in some states. The ABA also fears that the insurance industry would have an undue influence on the proposed payment schedule.

Procedural safeguards used to ensure fairness have not been addressed in the Health Court model.

The ABA prefers "sensible" reforms in the existing state tort systems but it is not clear what these "sensible" reforms would be.

So what is likely to happen with this proposed change in the medical malpractice tort resolution system? Under the present proposal, the Health Court system will probably be deemed unconstitutional. The burden of persuasion must be removed from the plaintiff to justify taking away his right to a trial. This could happen with a strict liability system.

Non-economic caps must be addressed in a way that would be deemed "fair" for all parties. Procedural safeguards need to be in place and the whole process must be immune from the effects of lobbyists.

In order to divorce these courts from outside influence, they should be deemed as Article III courts where the judges are appointed for life. An appeals process will need to be formulated using the Federal Courts of Appeal and, up to the Supreme Court if needed.

Under the Commerce Clause, the Congress has the power to regulate Commerce among the several states. Clearly medical malpractice is a commercial issue so Congress has the power to act in this area. Article III, Section 1 states, "[t]he judicial Power of the United States shall be vested in one Supreme Court, and in such inferior Courts as Congress may from time to time ordain and establish."[12] The Health Courts can be "such courts."

Judges in the Health Courts should be Article III judges with a life-time appointment. They could only be removed by impeachment for crimes and misdemeanors.

With these caveats, the proposed Health Court system could become a reality.

Of course, these courts could be allowed under Article V which describes the mechanism for amending the Constitution. This would be a difficult path to pursue since it requires 2/3 of both Houses or 2/3 of the state legislatures to propose the amendment. Once proposed, the amendment would then have to be ratified by ¾ of the States; not an easy task.[13]

Benefits of a Health Court System

- Quicker, more reliable justice.
- Improved patient safety.
- Lower costs.
- An open, trusting relationship with physicians.
- Liberalized compensation to cover avoidable injuries without the requirement of proving negligence. *ACS Bulletin May 2006*

Talk #2: Health Courts

Review, Recall, and Action

Citations

[11]Janice Mulligan, Chair of Standing Committee on Medical Professional Liability. 2006.
[12] United States Constitution Article III section 1.
[13] United States Constitution Article V.

Talk #3:
Stark Reality

In fiscal 2013, the rate of improper payments for Medicare services was 10.1%. This translates into $36 billion. This number was 8.5% ($29.6 billion) in 2012.[14] Health care costs are rising quickly in America; this rate of rise far exceeds the increase of the measured cost of living. Many feel that this rise is fueled by a pay for service model which dates back to Medicare and Medicaid which were instituted as part of the Great Society of Lyndon Johnson in 1964. Congress has long recognized the need to address improper payments as a means to mitigate these rising costs.

The Affordable Care Act has many provisions that are meant to curb the abuse inherent with this type of fee for service system.

In a fee for service model, it is not surprising that the providers might be inclined to increase the volume of their services so as to increase their income. In a Wall Street Journal editorial for December 12, 2013, Scott Gottlieb stated, "Everyone agrees that the system by which Medicare pays doctors is deeply flawed. It rewards doctors based on volume of services they deliver, with no measure of their quality of care... This creates all kinds of distortions in the market of medical care."

In an effort to curb some of this volume of what was felt to be unneeded health care, a law was passed in 1989 which was named after its writer, Pete Stark, a Democrat from California. The law went into effect on January 1, 1991. This was one of the first attempts to cut back on the number of referrals made, ostensibly to increase the income of providers. The first Stark law only applied to physician referrals of Medicare patients for clinical laboratory services. The original intent of the law was to prevent unethical referrals which were felt to be a prime driver of the increasing health care costs. Stark I only applied to physician referrals of Medicare patients for clinical laboratory services where the referring physician had a financial interest in the lab.

Stark I was originally meant to prevent physician self-referrals on Medicare claims only. Subsequently, case law developed which showed that self-referrals would not be allowed for both Medicare and Medicaid.

In 1993 and 1994, Congress expanded the prohibitions of self-referrals for other Designated Health Services (DHS). Stark II, a progeny of Stark I, extended the prohibitions to a broader range of health services, not just for clinical lab services where the referring practitioner had a "financial relationship." The list of prohibited referrals where the health care provider had a financial interest was extended to include clinical laboratory services, physical therapy services, occupational therapy services, radiology services (including MRI, CT scans, ultrasound services, and nuclear medicine), radiation therapy services and supplies, durable medical equipment and supplies, parenteral and enteral nutrients equipment and supplies, prosthetics, orthotics, and prosthetic devices and supplies, home health services, outpatient prescription drugs, and inpatient and outpatient hospitalization services.

The Stark laws basically limit the relationships into which a health care provider may enter. This is a complicated set of laws; the application is dependent on the facts of each individual situation.

In *US ex rel Baklid-Kunz v. Halifax Medical Center,* a hospital tried to argue that Stark was not violated because the providers were reimbursed by the State and not the Federal government.[15] The Court ruled against the hospital because the Federal government was reimbursing the State for the Medicaid payments. In fact, Medicaid payments are all initially made by the States which are then reimbursed, at some level, by the Federal government so in a roundabout way, the money was coming from the Feds. The final result of this ruling was that no Medicaid payments would be made to the states which have paid for DHS that were in violation of Stark.

Since the referrals could not be done if the practitioner had a "financial relationship" with the entity providing the services, it is important to know how "financial relationship" is defined. The practitioner may not have a direct ownership or investment interest or an indirect ownership or investment interest in the entity providing the services. There can be no direct or indirect compensation to the referring practitioner for the referral.

Examples of direct compensation to the practitioner include renting office space from a hospital, the hospital employing a physician, the hospital renting equipment from a physician, or a nursing home paying a physician as an independent contractor to serve as the nursing home's medical director. In all of these examples, there is the perception that the referring practitioner is being compensated for the referrals he is making to the entity providing the services.

In *Osheroff v. Tenet Healthcare Corp,* a realtor alleged that Tenet charged rent to physicians that was below fair market value to induce (and reward) physician referrals. If true, it would be a violation of Stark. The realtor sued under the theory that he could not compete with this unfair arrangement set up by Tenet. Tenet made a motion to dismiss because the Plaintiff had made no allegations of self-referral. The motion was denied as the Court concluded that Tenet may be liable under the False Claims Act since Tenet had previously certified they were compliant with all Medicare requirements. The penalties under the False Claims Act would have been severe so Tenet reached a settlement with the plaintiff that is pending approval by the Department of Justice.

In *Osheroff,* the Department of Justice got involved because they believed that Tenet caused the State of Florida to submit false claims to the federal government for services furnished on the basis of improper referrals.

To be liable for "indirect compensation," there has to be an unbroken chain between the provider and the entity to which he is referring. For example, if a physician owns stock in a "for profit" hospital and the hospital contracts with a clinical laboratory to provide services to the hospital's patients, an unbroken chain exists between the physician and the laboratory. Since the physician is likely to benefit financially from a referral, this would be a Stark violation.

A provider would also be in violation of Stark if any member of his "immediate family" were to benefit from a referral even if the provider were to realize no benefit to himself. The Stark law defines "immediate family" to include husband or wife, birth or adoptive parent, child, or sibling, stepparent, stepchild, stepbrother or stepsister, father-in-law, mother-in-law, brother-in-law, sister-in-law, grandparent or grandchild, and spouse of a grandparent or grandchild.

Stark has an interesting clause which actually forbids anyone from trying to get around the law so as to participate in the forbidden self-referrals. Any scheme or arrangement that has a principal purpose of assuring referrals by the practitioner to a particular entity to violate Stark is not allowed. Seems obvious, but attempts to get self-referrals still occur. Here is an example. Physicians A and B agree to refer their patients to the others diagnostic or treatment facility. This would be circumvention and is prohibited.

If a practitioner's compensation is dependent on the number or value of referrals, then this is a violation of Stark. A compensation arrangement may be excepted if it is for a personal services arrangement or is for "fair market value." It is common for hospitals to pay surgeons to take call so that the hospital can meet the requirements of the Emergency Medical Treatment and Active Labor Act (EMTALA). This would be allowed under the exception for personal services or for fair market value even though it looks like the hospital is paying the physician to refer patients to their hospital.

Stark is a noteworthy law due to the fact that there are numerous exceptions. Exceptions had to be made because there are many communities with very few health care providers and entities providing health care services. It would be unreasonable to have the patient travel hundreds of miles to get diagnostic tests if there was only one facility providing those services in the community and the physicians all had a financial interest in the facility.

In fact, there are so many exceptions to Stark, it takes a special health care lawyer to advise on what will be allowed under the circumstances of a particular case.

Only one of the exceptions is needed to permit what would otherwise constitute a prohibited referral. Remember, Stark only applies to referrals. It is not considered a "referral" if the DHS is personally performed by the referring physician. A surgeon who sees a patient in the clinic is allowed to send the patient to his hospital if he is going to do the case himself. Seems obvious, but it had to permitted as an exception or Stark would have been violated.

The penalties for Stark violations are numerous. There could be a denial of payment for the services provided; there could be a required refund of monies received by the entity for amounts already collected; there could be a payment of civil penalties ($15,000 for each service that a person "knows or should know" was provided in violation of the Stark law). There could also be a penalty of three times the amount received from Medicare.

There are penalties of up to $100,000 for each attempt to **circumvent** Stark. These penalties focus on cross referrals where the principal purpose is to assure referrals to a particular entity. These are really "indirect" referrals which the law was meant to prevent.

There is no jail time for violating Stark; however, there are several State laws which also forbid self-referrals and there may be jail time associated with those violations. The prosecutor may decide to bring charges involving Stark and State law; all the Stark penalties would be in play as would all the State penalties.

Under the Affordable Care Act, electronic medical records can be linked to income tax forms. A provider ordering tests can be linked to income from DHS that he has ordered. Computer programs can be written that would identify Stark violations based on the income tax records. Pretty clever!

Remember, Stark is a law with many exceptions. It has to be or it would be impossible to practice medicine. The way the law is written, it seems like any referral to colleagues in the group practice would be fraught with danger since it would be hard to prove that the referring practitioner had no "financial interest" in the referral. Recognizing this and other problems, Congress has made numerous exceptions where the law would not apply. These exceptions are what make the Stark law so complicated; this also allows some attorneys to make a good living.

Congress has made numerous exceptions where the Stark law would not apply. These exceptions are what make the Stark law so complicated; this also allows some attorneys to make a good living.

Stark only applies for Medicare and Medicaid beneficiaries and it only applies for referrals for Designated Health Services (DHS). DHS are defined. Believe it or not, lithotripsy is not a designated health service under Stark so a Urologist may legally refer his patient to his lithotripsy center even if he is not the one doing the procedure.

The list of what constitutes a DHS is long and includes clinical laboratory services, physical therapy, occupational therapy, and outpatient speech pathology services. Radiology and certain other imaging services are DHS unless they are integral to performing a medical procedure not identified with CPT codes as a radiology or imaging procedure. For example, an imaging procedure would be allowed immediately prior to or immediately after a medical procedure when it is necessary to confirm placement of an item placed during the procedure. This would include things like central lines, chest tubes, feeding tubes, and endotracheal tubes.

DHS which are part of a surgical bundle would be allowed. For example, if a coronary revascularization is done in a hybrid operating room where a LIMA is placed to the LAD (by a Cardiac Surgeon) and then PCI are done to other vessels (by a Cardiologist) this would be allowed under a Stark exception since it would all be billed as a bundle. However, you have to be careful to not unbundle as that would be considered billing fraud under other laws.

Requests by a pathologist for clinical diagnostic tests and pathologic examination services are not considered "referrals." Requests by a radiologist for diagnostic radiology services are not "referrals." Requests by a radiation oncologist for ancillary services needed for provision of radiation therapy are not "referrals."

Interestingly, if the provider writes an order for DHS **but does not direct where the Medicare beneficiary should receive the DHS,** this will not be considered as a "referral" even if there is a compensation relationship with the referring provider. It seems like this can occur with a wink and a nod so long as the patient plays along.

Academic medical centers have their own exceptions. Faculty physician compensation must be set in advance and cannot be related by the volume or value of the physician's referrals or other business generated within the academic medical center.

What about productivity bonuses? These will be allowed if they are based on DHS personally performed by the referring physician. For example: A physician who orders ultrasounds and then personally interprets the study may have his bonus tied to the number of ultrasounds he reads over the course of the year.

Productivity bonuses will also be allowed if they are directly based on DHS that are "incident to" services that the physician personally performed. A physician, for example, who performs a physical exam and then orders physical therapy based on the findings of the exam may have a bonus based on the provision of the physical therapy services.

A word of caution: Centers for Medicare and Medicaid (CMS) take the position that radiographs, lab tests, and other diagnostic tests can **never** be billed as "incidental to." Bonuses cannot be paid based on these types of tests unless the provider performed them himself.

To confuse matters even more, it is acceptable for productivity bonuses to be paid for DHS not personally performed or "incidental to" so long as it **is not directly related to** the volume or value of the physician's DHS referrals. For this to happen, the bonus must be based on the physician's **total** patient encounters. These DHS may not be payable by any other Federal program or private payer and it must be less than 5% of the practice's total revenue.

There is a physician recruitment exception for Stark which protects the remuneration that is provided by the hospital to recruit a physician to relocate into the area served by the hospital. This will not be looked on as "pay for referral." The Stark law will allow group practices to place restrictive covenants on their providers so long as the restrictions do not "unreasonably restrict" the recruited physician's ability to practice in the geographic area served by the hospital.

By law, the Veterans Administration may not bill Medicare for care it provides to veterans. Since Medicare cannot be billed, the VA is not subject to the Stark laws.

Hypothetical Scenario

There is an affiliation agreement between a private practice neurosurgery group and a medical school which calls for the group to "provide 'payment of overage'" to the college of medicine for neurosurgeons on the geographic full-time faculty of the Department of Neurosurgery. This payment will be based on a formula, "to be negotiated from time to time and will be related to the aggregate compensation of the full-time faculty." This agreement looks like the neurosurgery group will be "kicking back" some percentage of the payments received from work sent to them by the Medical school faculty. This is a kick-back scheme and there are several laws that forbid this type of arrangement. It is also a form of self-referral forbidden under Stark.

The Overwhelming Theme in Stark

The overwhelming theme in Stark, and other health care laws, is to cut costs by decreasing physician reimbursement; hospitals and other health care providers are also targeted for these cuts. Understanding the basics of the law will help keep the provider out of trouble since the penalties can be severe.

Stark is a complex law which the courts are still trying to sort out. Ignorance of the law is not a defense.

In 2014, the Senate Finance and the House Ways and Means Committees are working on ways to determine "applicable appropriate use criteria" for a full range of outpatient medical services delivered to Medicare patients. This will probably be extended to **all** care under the Affordable Care Act.

Within the Affordable Care Act is an Independent Payment Advisory Board (IPAB) whose mission is to find savings in Medicare without affecting coverage or quality. The IPAB has been granted authority to make changes; previously, Congress had to pass a law for changes to take effect. However, Congress will have the power to overrule the IPAB, but a supermajority will be required.

The IPAB must reduce payments to doctors, hospitals, and other providers. The IPAB is only minimally accountable to the President. The President can only remove a member for negligence or malfeasance. Other executive employees work at the "pleasure of the President." This is a huge change in the way things are run in Washington.

Constitutional issues have been raised with the authority of the IPAB.

- Can Congress give up power that it has been given in the Constitution?
- Remember, the Congress makes the law, the Executive enforces the law, and the Judicial branch says what the law is.

The Supreme Court will not get involved with this Constitutional issue until someone with "standing" brings a suit. This may not happen for many years. For the time being, the IPAB will not be subject to any significant oversight—judicial, Congress, or by the President.

In my opinion, this violates the "separation of powers" built into the Constitution, but it's hard to predict what the Supreme Court is likely to rule.

Be sure to have your own Health Care Attorney go over any contract that your practice is contemplating or involved in. Caution: Stark may be lurking.

Stark is a complex law which the courts are still trying to sort out. Ignorance of the law is not a defense.

Talk #3: Stark Reality

Review, Recall, and Action

Citations

[14] Adamy, Janet: Wall Street Journal, Red Flags in Medicare Billing. July 9, 2014.
[15] *US ex rel Baklid-Kunz v. Halifax Medical Center.*

Talk #4: Doctrine of Informed Consent

Consent to Surgery, Diagnostic Procedures, Transfusions or Other Medical/Dental Procedures

Patient Name: ______________________________

"I approve and direct Dr.(s) ______________________________________
or other doctors judged qualified by him or her to perform a
____."

Sign Here: ______________________________

?

How well do you understand Informed Consent?

Up until the 1970s, patients were inclined to let their physicians do whatever they thought was necessary to care for the patient. Patients generally loved their doctors and this reverence was a source of comfort. This respect for the physician was probably an important underpinning to the psychology of a cure.

> Ethicists have a lot to say about informed consent—"it's the right thing to do." Not surprisingly, what the law has to say about "informed consent," may have nothing to do with ethics.

With the Vietnam War and its associated anti-establishment views, along with the Consumer Movement of the 1970s, patients became more inclined to participate in their own health care decisions. They wanted more information presented in an understandable way. Why the change?

Previously, the physician-patient relationship was characterized by a large imbalance of power. The physician had superior knowledge and skill; the patient was vulnerable due to his illness and treatment. There were tremendous advances being made in medicine and surgery and there was a movement to increased specialization. Many physicians focused on financial gain since the pay structure had been switched (under the new Medicare and Medicaid laws) to a pay for procedure model. There was much money to be made.

Today, ethicists believe that getting a patient's informed consent is the right thing to do, but it was not always this way. Hippocrates said, "...conceal most things from the patient while you are attending him... revealing nothing of the patient's future or present condition." I doubt if Hippocrates would survive with those kinds of beliefs today.

In *Schloendorff v. Society of New York Hospital (1914),* the plaintiff had only consented to an exam under anesthesia. She specifically told the surgeon, a resident, there was to be no other procedures. During the exam, a tumor was found and the attending surgeon opted to remove it. Unfortunately, the patient developed gangrene in an arm.

She sued for damages. The wrong complained of was trespass, not negligence.

The trial court directed a verdict for the defendants. On appeal, since it was a directed verdict, the appellate court had to assume that the patient's narrative was true. With that as a baseline, they had to overrule the trial court. Justice Cardozo wrote the opinion of the appellate court. He noted that it is a fundamental concept in American Jurisprudence that "[e]very human being of adult years and sound mind has a right to determine what shall be done with his own body... "[16] He went on to say, "... and a surgeon who performs an operation without his patient's consent commits an assault, for which he is liable in damages."[17]

In the 1970s, this concept was rediscovered. "It is the settled rule that therapy not authorized by the patient may amount to a tort—a common law battery—by the physician."[18]

The Doctrine of Informed Consent was established in the states to help restore the patient's individual autonomy. It requires the practitioner to provide information to the patient to redress the power imbalance created by the inequality of knowledge inherent in present day health care.

> Informed consent is a process whereby the health care practitioner tells the patient what a reasonable patient needs to know to make a decision as to consent.

The legal dimensions of informed consent are centered in the right to privacy and the law of battery. Although the right to privacy is not explicitly stated in the Constitution of the United States, the Justices say it is in there somewhere.[19]

The tort of battery deals with the concept that any unpermitted contact or offensive touching is a personal indignity. As such, the patient has a right to have the information needed to make an intelligent, informed choice about whether to accept or reject medical recommendations.

States have police power to ensure the general welfare. Informed consent has been deemed to be an important state interest in ensuring the general welfare and, as a result, all states have either thru common law or statute, made rules as to what is required in getting an informed consent from a patient prior to doing any treatment or procedure.

In *Shadrick v. Coker,* a patient had several operations done on the spine without success. Finally, hardware was placed on the spine to provide stability and fuse the vertebrae. The fusion was done in March 1990. In November 1990, one of the spinal screws broke and had to be removed. Back pain was constant for this patient.

In December 1993, a segment is shown on ABC's *20/20,* which is an expose on the pedicle screws of the spinal device that was the same device that had been used on Mr. Shadrick. The show pointed out that the screws were experimental and that they were failing at a high rate. In December 1994, Shadrick brings suit alleging medical malpractice, lack of informed consent, and battery.[20]

The trial court in *Shadrick* grants the defendant's motion for summary judgment. The Court of Appeals reverses his ruling, finding that there were disputed issues of material fact as to when Shadrick should have discovered his cause of action. The Supreme Court of Tennessee took the case and affirmed the Court of Appeals.

In Tennessee, informed consent depends on what a reasonable patient would need to know in order to make a reasonable decision. This is a question for the jury to decide and does *not* require any expert testimony; the jury should have the knowledge and experience to make this decision without any help from expert testimony. However, the information that needs to be presented to the patient does require expert testimony as to what a reasonable practitioner would convey if faced with the same or similar circumstances.

So what does a patient need to know? In Tennessee, it is required that the patient be told his diagnosis or the nature of his ailment, the reasons for the proposed treatment or procedure, the risks involved and the prospects for success, and alternative methods of treatment along with the risks and benefits of such treatment. The patient must also be told if the treatment is experimental.

Whether the information given to the patient is sufficient for him to make an informed consent, "depends on the nature of the treatment, the extent of the risks involved, and the standard of care."[21]

The burden of proof is on the plaintiff. He must prove, by expert testimony, that the defendant did not provide the appropriate information so that an informed consent could be made.

There are two standards used by the states in determining informed consent. In the *objective patient standard,* the physician must disclose what a reasonable patient needs to know in order to give an informed consent. He must give the information needed to enable an intelligent choice. This is the standard used in Tennessee. It is also the standard used in the *1992 Code of Medical Ethics* used by the American Medical Association. However, this is the minority standard used in the country.

The standard used by most states is the *professional disclosure standard.* Here the practitioner must disclose what a reasonably prudent practitioner would disclose under the same or similar circumstances. This standard may be met even if it does not provide the patient with the information he needs to make an intelligent decision. Expert testimony is required as the jury will not know what the standard of care is for the professional.

In a recent case, a coronary angioplasty was done on a diabetic patient with a poor result. He brought suit based on lack of informed consent since the surgical option was never mentioned by the cardiologist. Plaintiff's expert needed to only answer one question:

"Could bypass surgery have been a reasonable option for this patient?"

Since his opinion was that surgery was a reasonable option, the lack of informed consent became the main cause of action.

Most, if not all hospitals, have an informed consent document that they make the patient sign before any procedure. This document is not consent but it is evidence that the informed consent process did occur. Consent lies in the conclusion of the discussion between the patient and the practitioner where the required elements of consent were addressed.

If there is no informed consent document signed by the patient in the chart, a note by the practitioner who participated in the consent process can be used as evidence that informed consent was obtained.

Consent lies in the conclusion of the discussion between the patient and the practitioner where the required elements of consent were addressed... Only the practitioner is competent to explain the risks and benefits for that particular patient.

The hospital does *not* have an independent duty to obtain the consent. Only the practitioner is competent to explain the risks and benefits for that particular patient. However, the hospital may have some **vicarious liability** for a practitioner's breach of the duty to obtain informed consent if it **knows** the practitioner is not fulfilling his duty to obtain the informed consent. The hospital may also have some vicarious liability if the practitioner is an employee of the hospital and the hospital controls the practice in some way.

The question has been raised as to the assumption of a duty by the hospital by having a requirement that an informed consent document be signed by the patient. In fact, it is often a nurse who is not involved with the procedure who has the patient sign the document. The courts that have addressed this issue have decided that the forms were not designed to replace the informed consent process required of the practitioner and, as such, the hospital was not gratuitously assuming the duty to obtain the consent.

This issue has been codified in some states. For example, in Idaho the hospital may perform the ministerial act of documenting such consent, but the practitioner himself must do the process of obtaining the informed consent.[22] Absent the assumption, the hospital will not be liable for malpractice. The hospital cannot assume the physician's (practitioner's) "non-delegable" duty. The surgeon who tells the nurse to get the consent is looking for trouble.

Some lawyers have said that the absence of the informed consent document in the medical record equates to no informed consent at all. This may not be true. Consent may have been obtained and the courts will allow oral testimony to prove it. Valid consent is to be gleaned from the circumstances and discussions surrounding the consent process.[23]

So who is responsible for obtaining the patient's consent? At a hospital in Memphis, a nurse was trained to put in peripherally inserted central lines (PICC). She asked the Surgery Service to get the informed consent before she would place the lines. The Surgical Service refused. The Chief of Surgery opined that the person performing the procedure was the one required to get the consent.

Historically, the physician had the duty to get consent since the courts felt they were in the best position to discuss the care and management with the patient. However, as more procedures were being done by other health care providers, the responsibility shifted to the provider doing the procedure; that person may not be the physician. Hospital policy now requires that the practitioner who will perform the treatment or procedure must ensure that the informed consent process is followed.

In fact, hospital policy usually defines the practitioner to be any physician, dentist, or health care professional who has been granted specific clinical privileges to perform the treatment or procedure. Is a nurse a health care professional? They sure are.

In general, the courts do not want the hospitals to get involved in issues that lie at the heart of the doctor-patient relationship.

There are defenses that the practitioner can raise if insufficient disclosure in the consent process is alleged. These defenses include (1) waiver of informed consent, (2) therapeutic privilege, (3) religious, cultural, or ethnic issues, (4) emergencies, and (5) implied consent.

Some patients do not want any information and prefer that the physician does whatever he feels is best. The patient may waive his right to informed consent but only if he gives the waiver **knowingly.** The **knowing** requirement implies some duty of disclosure on the practitioner's part. It is not clear how much disclosure needs to be done and it is not certain that the waiver be in writing.

On occasion, it may not be in the patient's best interest to get the needed information for an informed consent to occur. This is a physician decision and is deemed to be a therapeutic privilege. Some state statutes and some judicial opinions recognize this defense. Plaintiff's attorneys dislike this defense because they believe it destroys the general duty to disclose. If this defense is used, an objective standard will probably be used to determine if the physician was reasonable.

What if death and dying are forbidden topics for the patient? This may be a religious, cultural, or ethnic issue. Some religious groups prefer physician beneficence over patient autonomy. It is usually best to get a waiver from the patient rather than assuming that this is a justification for withholding the necessary information needed to make an informed consent.

Sometimes the physician knows something that the patient wishes to keep confidential such as HIV status. That patient may present in an unconscious state due to trauma. What information must the physician reveal to the decision maker so that an informed consent can be given? The HIV status is clearly relevant. In this type of situation, the states, often by statute, give the duly appointed agent an absolute right to **all** of the patient's medical information. The surrogate's right to know trumps the practitioner's obligation for confidentiality.

In medical emergencies where the patient is in no condition to participate in the consent process and there is no one available to give the consent on his behalf, then the provider is given the go-ahead to do what he thinks is right. There is a strong public interest in providing the care under these circumstances, even without the consent.

There are instances where the patient may not be able to give consent at the time of the treatment but his consent could be implied. There was a recent study performed where *stroma free hemoglobin,* a blood substitute, was being used in trauma patients. The community was informed prior to the study being started and the people could opt out of the study by putting a special band on their steering wheel. Trauma victims without the band were entered into the study whether they wanted to be part of it or not. Obviously, this is a contentious area of the law which has not yet been clarified.

Another area of *implied consent* is in the operating room where the surgeon discovers a problem different from the one that consent was given to treat. In this scenario, the surgeon will usually break scrub to go and talk to the family. Hopefully, the family will agree for him to proceed. However, if there are no surrogates readily available, the surgeon works under this *implied consent* to do what he thinks is best for the patient. Again, there is a strong public interest to let the surgeon do what he thinks is best for the patient under these circumstances.

What if the patient does not give the practitioner complete information that may be material to the case? For example, if the patient uses illegal drugs and hides that information, the risks discussed may not be complete or accurate because the practitioner does not have this critical information. In a *comparative negligence* state, like Tennessee, the patient may have some liability if he is injured. In fact, if the patient's negligence is greater than 50%, then the practitioner may win the case even if he had some liability also.

In summary, *informed consent* is a process whereby the health care practitioner tells the patient what a reasonable patient needs to know to make an informed decision as to consent. In Tennessee, the practitioner will be held to a "reasonable practitioner" standard for like or similar circumstances in the same or similar community. Check with your attorney for the standard your state follows in its Doctrine of Informed Consent.

Talk #4: Doctrine of Informed Consent

Review, Recall, and Action

Citations

[16] *Schloendorff v. Society of New York Hospital,* 105 N.E. 92, 93 (1914)
[17] Id.
[18] *Canterbury v. Spence,* 464 F.2d 772 (D.C. Cir) (1972)
[19] The Supreme Court has stated that this right is evident in the penumbra (shadowed regions) formed by emanations from the Bill of Rights in the 1st, 3rd, 4th, 5th, and 9th amendments)
[20] "Battery" is an unwanted, offensive touching
[21] *Cardwell,* 724 S.W.2d at 749
[22] Idaho Code sec.39-4306
[23] *Kovacs v. Freeman,* 957 S.W.2d 251 (Ky. 1997)

Talk #5:
Futility

Advanced Care Directive * Power of Attorney * Living Will

Health care providers are occasionally faced with a situation where the patient or his surrogate demands care that the provider believes to be futile (medically inappropriate). Although State law seems to provide some protection for the provider, there is still a reluctance to go against the wishes of the patient or surrogate for fear of a civil suit based on medical malpractice, wrongful death, or lack of informed consent. There are also fears of criminal charges up to and including murder.

These fears are justified based on the vagueness of the state statutes, the potential for federal pre-emption, and the possibility that the statutes may be unconstitutional based on the lack of "due process" as required in the Fourteenth Amendment.

By formulating a process that the health care provider can use when faced with a situation where futile care is being requested by the patient or surrogate, time and information can be used to convince the requester that, perhaps, comfort measures may be the most reasonable medical option for their loved one.

By formulating a process that the health care provider can use when faced with a situation where futile care is being requested by the patient or surrogate, time and information can be used to convince the requester that, perhaps, comfort measures may be the most reasonable medical option for their loved one.

The goal of the process is to seek agreement between the provider and the surrogate. The process will involve:

1. Informing the surrogate of the intent to withhold or withdraw care. This will provide the surrogate with notice of the proposed action so that he is aware of the intent of the providers. No care will be withheld or withdrawn while the surrogate is formulating his response.
2. Getting a second opinion from another provider that agrees with the first provider. The surrogate will be informed of the results of this second opinion.
3. Obtaining a consult from the hospital's Medical Ethics Committee. The opinion of this committee will be made known to the surrogate.
4. If the surrogate is still not in agreement with the providers, then efforts to transfer the patient to a provider who is willing to go with the care being requested by the surrogate will be made.

If a transfer is not possible, only then will a unilateral decision to withdraw or withhold care be made. While the process is ongoing, care will be provided to the patient that is consistent with the requests of the surrogate.

> The goal of the process is to seek agreement between the provider and the surrogate.

The Theresa Schiavo case is an example of how complex these types of cases may become. Schiavo was happily married and employed. On February 25, 1990, at age 27, she suffered a cardiac arrest as a result of a potassium imbalance. Her husband called 911 and she was rushed to the hospital. She never regained consciousness.

A medical negligence suit was brought and Schiavo won a substantial amount. There was an out of court settlement with one physician for $250,000 and there was a jury award (after lawyer's fees) of $300,000 for her husband, Michael, and $750,000 in trust for Theresa's medical care.

In May of 1998, eight years after this tragedy began Michael petitioned the guardianship court to authorize the termination of life-prolonging procedures. Theresa's parents, Robert and Mary Schindler, opposed this petition. There was no living will or power of attorney. This difficult decision was thus placed in the hands of the court.

There are associated confounding facts. Michael by then had a girlfriend with whom he had a child. Michael could divorce Theresa, but then any funds remaining from the malpractice award, at Theresa's death, would likely go to the parents.

After a hearing at which Michael and the Schindler's presented evidence, the guardianship court issued an extensive written order authorizing the discontinuance of artificial life support.

The court used a clear and convincing evidence standard.[24] The court found that Theresa Schiavo was in a persistent vegetative state (PVS) and that Theresa would elect to cease life-prolonging procedures if she were competent to make her own decision.

The Schindlers appealed; the appellate court affirmed the lower court. The Florida Supreme court denied review.[25]

In its opinion, the appellate court stated, "Medicine cannot cure this condition. Unless an act of God, a true miracle, was to recreate her brain, Theresa will always remain in an unconscious, reflexive state, totally dependent upon others to feed her and care for her most private needs. She could remain in this state for many years."

The court, in making its decision, was putting itself in Theresa's situation; whether Theresa would choose to continue the constant nursing care and the supporting tubes in hopes that a miracle would recreate her missing brain tissue, or whether she would prefer a natural death process to take its course and for her family members and loved ones to be free to continue with their lives.

There are two standards that the courts use in making this type of difficult decision. The *subjective standard* requires the court to do what an incompetent person would do if he were competent to make the decision. There must be clear evidence available, usually from past conversations when the person was competent, upon which to base this decision.

The other standard, the *objective standard,* is used when there is no trustworthy evidence available of the ward's desire. What would a reasonable person do in the same or similar circumstances? The trial judge, based on testimony of witnesses, felt he had clear and convincing evidence of what Theresa would have decided if she were competent.

The Schindlers filed a motion for relief from the judgment which is allowed under the Florida rules of Civil Procedure. They alleged that there was newly discovered evidence and intrinsic fraud. They also filed a challenge to the final judgment in the guardianship court.[26] The court ruled that the motion was untimely.

On appeal, the Second District agrees that the denial of the motion was correct, but they also rule that the Schindlers may institute an independent action whereby they can challenge the original judgment on the grounds that it is "no longer equitable for the trial court to enforce its earlier order." In order to win this challenge, the Schindlers would have to prove that Theresa would not have made the decision to withdraw life-prolonging procedures fourteen months earlier when the final order was entered, or she would make a different decision now based on subsequent developments.

The motion is initiated and the trial court quickly denies it. The appeals court reverses the trial court and sends the case back to the guardianship court for the purpose of conducting a limited evidentiary hearing on the alleged "new evidence" that a new treatment could dramatically improve Theresa's condition and allow her to recover some cognitive function.

The guardianship court hears the evidence and then denies the motion for relief from the previous judgment. On appeal, the Second District affirms. On this, its fourth opinion on this case, the court states, "It may be unfortunate that when families cannot agree, the best forum we can offer for this private, personal decision is a public courtroom and the best decision-maker we can provide is a judge with no prior knowledge of the ward, but the law currently provides no better solution that adequately protects the interests of promoting the value of life."

On October 15, 2003, Theresa's nutrition and hydration tube is removed. On October 21st, the Florida legislature steps in and enacts a new law which Governor Jeb Bush quickly signs. The law stays the continued withholding of nutrition for Ms. Schiavo. The feeding tube is reinserted.

This was clearly a separation of powers issue, a basic tenet of the Florida Constitution. A legislature may not delegate its legislative powers to the governor. Also, "...statutes granting power to the executive branch must clearly announce adequate standards to guide... in the execution of the powers delegated."

The Florida legislature had essentially given Governor Jeb Bush the power to be a law giver rather than the administrator of the law, at least in regard to Theresa

Schiavo. He had unfettered discretion to decide whether to issue and when to lift a *stay* which makes his decision virtually unreviewable by any other branch.

The new law pertaining to Theresa Schiavo did not even require the Governor to consider the patient's wishes in deciding whether to issue a stay on withholding of life-prolonging procedures. There was no due process for Theresa Schiavo in regard to this new law.[27]

Was Ms. Schiavo a "person?" Was she even alive?

In 1868 when the Fourteenth Amendment went into effect, a person was considered dead when the heart stopped beating and respirations also stopped. Today, whole brain death (cortex and brain stem) is now accepted by most states as death. New York and New Jersey still require irreversible cessation of the circulatory system and respiratory function for the person to be declared dead.

Whole brain death is easy to diagnose. Upper brain death is difficult to diagnose. Theresa was felt to have upper brain death.

Upper brain death is a clinical diagnosis made on repeated physical exams; it is not made by laboratory studies. These patients may laugh, cry, grimace, yawn, swallow, and open the eyes, all as involuntary reflexes controlled by the brain stem. Scans of the brain are known to have both false positives and false negatives.

The American Medical Association's position on upper brain death, also called persistent vegetative state (PVS), is that these patients are not dead, but it is ethical, under certain conditions, to withdraw care. Most States consider these patients as persons to whom care can be given or not, depending on that patient's expressed desires made during their conscious life.

There is no federal definition of personhood but the word "person" appears in 16 clauses of the Constitution. In fact, it appears three times in the Fourteenth Amendment alone.

Each state is free to make its own interpretation of personhood. As medical costs rise, it is conceivable that some states may deny "personhood" to the terminally ill or the severely disabled. The Tenth Amendment seems to reserve this power to the states. A person with PVS may be a "person" in one state but not another.

Michael Schiavo moves for a declaratory judgment in the circuit court and on May 6, 2004, the circuit court enters a judgment in favor of Michael. The Court notes that the Florida statute was unconstitutional on its face and, as applied to Theresa Schiavo, an unlawful delegation of legislative authority and a violation of her right to privacy. It was unconstitutional as applied because it allowed the Governor to encroach upon the judicial power and to retroactively abolish Theresa's vested right to privacy.

The Court states, "When the prescribed procedures are followed according to our rules of court and the governing statutes, a final judgment is issued, and all post-judgment procedures are followed, it is without question an invasion of the authority of the judicial branch for the legislature to pass a law that allows the executive branch to interfere with the final judicial determination of a case."

It would seem that this ruling would be final, but it was not. The United States Congress steps in by enacting Public Law No. 109-3 which would allow the Federal Courts to re-hear the case essentially from scratch. Theresa's parents try to get a temporary restraining order to get the feeding tube replaced so that the Federal courts can re-hear the case while Theresa is still alive.

The issue of the Temporary Restraining Order (TRO) was raised while Congress was working on the Act. Bill Frist, the Senator from Tennessee, felt that the TRO issue did not need to be addressed. He said, "Nothing in the current bill mandates a stay. I would assume… the court would grant a stay… because Mrs. Schiavo would need to be alive in order for the court to make its determination." This assumption turned out to be a critical mistake. Some say that the Congress made this mistake on purpose to give the courts an out to avoid the Constitutional issues.

In order for the TRO to be granted, the requesting party bears the burden to clearly establish four prerequisites. They would need to prove a substantial likelihood of success on the merits of the case, irreparable injury if the injunction is not granted, the threatened injury to the party requesting the injunction outweighs the potential damage that the proposed injunction may cause the defendants, and that the injunction would not be adverse to the public interest.

The last three prerequisites were easy for Theresa's parents to prove. They were to lose on the first requirement. The District Court held that the movants failed to demonstrate that they were likely to win if the case were to be reheard in its entirety. Therefore, there would be no TRO to replace the feeding tube to allow the Federal court time to revisit the case.

On appeal, the District Court was affirmed based on an abuse of discretion standard. The appellate court wrote, "We also conclude that the district court's carefully thought-out decision to deny temporary relief in these circumstances is not an abuse of discretion."

Theresa dies shortly thereafter and that essentially ended the "case or controversy" as far as the court was concerned. Without a "case or controversy," there was no reason for any federal court to re-hear the issues. As a result, the constitutional issues were not definitively resolved.

Stare decisis is a doctrine of precedent under which it is necessary for courts to follow earlier judicial decisions when the same or similar points are raised again in litigation. The proposed re-hearing of the Schiavo case by the Federal courts was more than just "the same points;" it was the same case which had been already decided and affirmed after an exhaustive appeals process. It is no wonder that the courts were upset with both the legislative and executive branches for over-reaching into the court's domain. They viewed this as a breach of the separation of powers written into the Constitution.

Remember, Theresa was not brain-dead. The autopsy confirmed that she was in a persistent vegetative state. Did the judge, or doctor, or family have the right to stop her care? By what standards must individuals be judged to warrant removal of life-dependent care?

Theresa's gravestone marker states the following:
Beloved Wife
Born December 3, 1963
Departed This Earth February 25, 1990
At Peace March 31, 2005
I Kept My Promise

It is said that societies are judged by how they protect their most vulnerable members. How should we determine from whom to withhold or withdraw care if we do not know the patient's wishes? What about assisted suicide? This is permitted in Oregon and the Federal courts have allowed this to stand.

Clearly the bar has been lowered. Care can be withdrawn from brain-dead patients and from patients with *persistent vegetative states*. Can care be withdrawn or withheld from patients with terminal illness, or senile dementia, or Alzheimer's? All of these issues are heavily fact-dependent and I could find no clear answer other than to treat them under the particular state's futility statute.

The right to die was first addressed in the 1990 case of *Cruzan v. Director, Missouri Department of Health.*[28] The Missouri court held that the courts could insist on proof by a "*clear and convincing* evidence standard of a comatose patient's desire to terminate her life before allowing her family's wish to disconnect her feeding tube." The right to die, according to Missouri, was a liberty protected by the Due Process Clause. However, this court did not address the right to *assisted suicide.*

The Uniform Health Care Decisions Act of 1993 requires a guardian to comply with a ward's previously given instructions, and prohibits a guardian from revoking the ward's advance health-care directive without the court's express approval. There is also the right to refuse health care; this was deemed a liberty interest which is protected under the Constitution.

Although the Supreme Court affirmed Cruzan had a right to refuse medical care, it also held that there was no constitutional right for assisted suicide. This left it for the states to decide on this issue. Oregon's decision to allow assisted suicide (with strict controls) has been upheld on several court challenges.

On the other side, criminal laws against physician-assisted suicide in Washington and New York were found to be constitutional in 1997.

I am not sure that the courts are the best venue to decide these societal issues. The opinions of the courts on these issues are often based on the personal perspectives of a few individuals who, at least in the Federal system, are not elected. I believe that the legislative bodies (Federal and state) are best situated to utilize task forces to conduct hearings on these issues, and their decisions can be checked by the electorate. As Justice Brandeis noted in *New State Ice Co. v. Liebmann,* "[t]he ability of states to function as 'laboratories' for social experiments is one of the happy incidents of the federal system."[29]

- Assisted suicide is allowed in Oregon;
- Kevorkian served years in prison for second degree murder;
- Withdrawal of care is allowed for brain-dead patients or patients in persistent vegetative states;
- Abortion is allowed if the fetus is not yet viable outside of the uterus (not yet a person).

Who should we treat and how much treatment should we do? All are difficult concepts with many differences of opinion in the country.

In the Schiavo case, the courts dodged the larger constitutional issues; they did nothing to change the rules as they presently stand. Even the Congress, by writing the Schiavo statute so narrowly, was able to avoid the constitutional issues. I believe they did this on purpose. Their constituents were appeased but nothing much was accomplished.

All of these issues are difficult for providers who are the ones on the front line dealing with them. Dialogue must continue if we are ever to get meaningful solutions.

For now, health care providers should do what they can to make sure their patients have an advanced directive as to health care issues before they become unable to make a decision. Living wills and powers of attorney for health care issues would also be helpful. Perhaps these issues can be addressed up front by state statutes which can make them mandatory for such things like driver's licenses or voter registration. In many states, organ donor decisions are already part of statutory law and are part of the driver's license.

There is much work to be done on these difficult and contentious health care issues.

> It is said that societies are judged
> by how they protect
> their most vulnerable members.

Talk #5: Futility

Review, Recall, and Action

Citations

[24] Evidence indicating that the thing to be proved is highly probable or reasonably certain; this is a greater burden than preponderance of the evidence, the standard applied in most civil cases, and less than evidence beyond a reasonable doubt, the norm for criminal trials

[25] In *re Guardianship of Schiavo*, 789 So. 2d 348 (Fla. 2001)

[26] 792 So.2d 551 (Fla. 2d DCA 2001)

[27] The Fourteenth Amendment says in part "…nor shall any State deprive any person of life, liberty, or property, without due process of law…"

[28] *Cruzan v. Director, Missouri Department of Health.*

[29] 285 U.S. 262, 311 (1982)

Talk #6: Resident Personnel Files: Are They Discoverable?

A recent malpractice case was brought against some members of the Department of Surgery at the University of Tennessee. A surgical resident was also a named defendant. The plaintiff's attorney subpoenaed the resident's personnel file in hopes of finding some incriminating evidence that would show negligent hiring, privileging, or supervision of this particular resident.

Taken by surprise, the Chairman of Surgery surrendered the file without getting input from legal counsel. The Associate Dean of Graduate Medical Education thought that this surrender was a mistake so he requested a legal opinion.

There were basically three arguments that could be used to keep the resident personnel files out of plaintiff's hands.

The first argument relies on the Family Educational Rights and Privacy Act of 1974 (FERPA). The intent of this law is to protect a student's right to privacy by "limiting the transferability [and disclosure] of their records without their consent." If the records are released without the proper consent, the Department of Education may discontinue funding to that educational institution.

The problem with using the FERPA argument is found in section 99.31(9)(i) of the law. This section points out that disclosure does not require prior consent if the disclosure is to comply with a judicial order or **lawfully issued subpoena.** Since the University was responding to a subpoena in the first place, this argument was a loser from the start.

The second argument deals with relevance of the information in the files. Rules of Civil Procedure limit discovery to matters relevant to the subject matter involved in the pending action. It's conceivable that there would be information in the resident's file relating to competence, standard of care on a particular case, and privileges. If the plaintiff was looking to add on a negligent hiring or negligent privileging cause of action, then clearly the files could have relevant information. It would not be a good argument to claim lack of relevance in trying to keep the files out; claiming a privilege is the better way to go and this is the route the University of Tennessee eventually took.

This request for a resident's file had never happened before at this medical school. The Accreditation Counsel for Graduate Medical Education had no policy on this issue. There was no statute in Tennessee protecting these particular documents. Even if there was a privilege protecting these documents, the privilege was lost when the files were released to the Plaintiff, at least for this particular case.

Under Tennessee Rules of Evidence, Article V describes privileges by which a person may refuse to produce an object or writing that has been requested by an opposing attorney.[30] Examples of these privileges include: Doctor-Patient, Lawyer-Client, and Husband-Wife. These types of relationships have been deemed to be so confidential that the state feels this confidentiality should not be breeched, even with a subpoena.

Legal counsel thought that the Tennessee Peer Review Statute may apply. This statute describes a privilege which should encourage Tennessee's licensed physicians to "candidly, conscientiously, and objectively evaluate and review their peers professional conduct, competence, and ability to practice medicine."[31]

Perhaps a group faculty meeting to evaluate residents was comparable to a "peer review committee" which was recognized to have a privilege to keep records emanating from the committee privileged. This was the strategy adopted by the University to keep resident personnel files out to the hands of plaintiffs in future cases.

In Tennessee and several other states, a "peer review privilege" is recognized whereby the quality of health care delivered is evaluated by peers of a provider. The privilege is known as the "Medical Review Committee-Informant Privilege." This privilege applies to a "peer review committee... the function of which, or one of the functions of which, is to evaluate and improve the quality of health care rendered by providers..."[32]

The committee will also determine if the standard of care has been met. This process allows all who participate to learn from mistakes of others and to take steps to see that those mistakes are not made again.

In *Stratienko, MD v. Chattanooga-Hamilton County Hospital Authority et al,* the Tennessee Supreme Court held that "the information, documents, or records otherwise available from original sources are subject to discovery pursuant to Tennessee Code Annotated section 63-6-219(e), but only to the extent that they are not requested from the peer review committee and are not otherwise privileged."[33]

In *Stratienko,* appellee Stratienko was trying to discover the "peripheral vascular credentials" of another physician with whom he had a physical altercation. Because of the fight, Stratienko had his hospital privileges suspended and he was trying to get those privileges back. The court held that the information being sought was privileged.

Did *Stratienko* or the "peer review privilege" apply to the resident personnel file? Are residents even considered to be "licensed physicians?" Are residents "peers" of the attendings, or are attendings "peers" of the residents? Is a group of faculty members a true "peer review committee"? These questions had never been addressed by the Tennessee courts, so there was no precedent on which to rely.

There was a Texas case on point but it could not be used as precedent outside of that state. In *Garza v. Scott and White Memorial Hospital,* a resident was being sued for malpractice.[34] The plaintiff was hoping to show that the hospital was negligent for credentialing this particular resident and they needed the personnel files to support this claim. The Federal District Court held that the resident evaluations were privileged under the Texas Peer Review Statute.[35]

Stratienko and Garza became the models for the University of Tennessee to claim the peer review privilege for the next case where a plaintiff subpoenaed a resident's file.

In arguing for the privilege, there is a strong public interest in training competent physicians who can take care of patients safely and independently. Training would be impaired if attendings could not evaluate residents in confidence; this is what would occur if the records of the meeting were subject to discovery. Attendings would be wary of being critical if they were afraid that their statements could be read back to them at a later time in a court of law.

Because of these incidents, the University of Tennessee lobbied to get new laws passed by the state legislature which would make the resident's files privileged. They were successful. The faculties of the medical schools in the state are now considered to each be a Peer Review Committee when they perform resident evaluations. The findings of this committee, entered into the resident's personnel file are now protected from a subpoena from plaintiff's attorneys. [36]

Claiming a privilege is just the first step in a legal process for withholding requested information. Under most states' Rules of Civil Procedure, the withholding party must inform the requesting party that information is being withheld. Enough information must be given so that the requesting party can make a determination if the privilege claimed is applicable. If there is disagreement on the applicability of the claimed privilege, the court may have to hear arguments and make a decision as to whether the claimed privilege is justified under the law.

This was a great example of the legal process functioning in a way that would benefit our ability to train future physicians. One of the missions of the University of Tennessee, typical for a Land Grant University, is to enhance the health care of the citizens for the State of Tennessee. Only through candid discussions can the faculty of the medical school critically evaluate and improve the performance of the residents. This will ultimately improve the quality of care for future generations of the citizens of the state.

> Claiming a privilege is just the first step in a legal process for withholding requested information…
> If there is disagreement on the applicability of the claimed privilege, the court may have to hear arguments and make a decision as to whether the claimed privilege is justified under the law.

Talk #6: Resident Personnel Files: Are They Discoverable?

Review, Recall, and Action

Citations

[30]Tennessee Rules of Evidence, Article 5: Privileges, Rule 501 (1990).
[31] T.C.A. Section 63-6-219(e).
[32] Tennessee Peer Review Law, Tenn. Code Ann. Section 63-219(c) (1967).
[33] *Alexander A. Stratienko, MD, v. Chattanooga-Hamilton County Hospital Authority, et al,* No. E2005-01043-SC-S09-CV-filed May 14, 2007.
[34] *Garza v. Scott and White Memorial Hospital,* 234 F.R.D. 617 (2005).
[35] Texas Health and Safety Code, Section 161.032.
[36] Tennessee Code Annotated, Section 68-11-272. This is now known as the "Tennessee Patient Safety and Quality Improvement Act of 2011." Tennessee Code Annotated, Section 63-1-150 became effective April 8, 2014. This law further protects the Quality Improvement Committee (QIC) by securing record confidentiality.

Talk #7:
Themes for Malpractice Defense

Ignorance of the Law and How It Operates Is No Defense

During the course of a physician's career, the odds are high that he will be named in a medical malpractice suit. In Tennessee, for example, a cardiac surgeon will be named in a malpractice action on average, once every three years. In an effort to better handle the stresses of being sued, knowledge of legal strategies would be helpful.

In order to win a malpractice suit, the plaintiff must prove that the defendant;

1. Owed a duty of care to the plaintiff;
2. The defendant acted negligently in providing that care, and;
3. The plaintiff was injured as a result of the negligent care, i.e., the proximate cause of the injury was the negligent care.

The level of proof required is "preponderance of the evidence." This means more likely than not or a greater than 50% likelihood.

If the plaintiff fails to prove all three elements by a preponderance of the evidence standard, then the defendant will win (by law).

Before any state actor ("actor" is a legal term implying that the party is acting as an agent of the state) can take someone's life, liberty, or property, due process of law must occur. This is a requirement of the United States Constitution. "Due process" means that the defendant must be notified of the pending legal action and he must have a fair hearing on the merits of the case.

Being served with papers is usually the first thing that happens to a defendant in a medical malpractice case. When papers are served, the defendant should notify his malpractice carrier as soon as possible. There is a time limit on making an answer to the plaintiff's allegations; the more time your attorney has in formulating the response the better.

Sometimes it may be prudent to settle the case. This is especially true if it appears that the plaintiff has a good case for malpractice and the harm done was significant. The following is an example of such a case.

A Medical Malpractice Case

On July 15, 2003, Courtney Hill, 23 years old, called her OB/Gyn because she felt a lump in her breast that had persisted for two months. "Should I come in immediately?" she asked. The nurse in the office asked the physician, Dr. Moise, if a mammogram should be ordered.

Dr. Moise did not see a need for a mammogram and she scheduled an appointment for two weeks later. At the time of the office visit, Dr. Moise examined the lump and told Courtney that the mass was "a cyst or fatty deposit" and "nothing to worry about." No ultrasound, mammogram, or other testing was ordered by Dr. Moise, and no follow up visit was arranged. Surprisingly, there was no documentation of Dr. Moise's findings in the medical record and no reminder to check the mass at a later date.

Courtney subsequently got pregnant. She was seen by Dr. Moise on 16 different visits without any further evaluation or testing of the breast mass. Dr. Moise admitted that Courtney kept every appointment and followed every recommendation during the pregnancy.

Dr. Moise admitted that there was no follow up of the breast mass.

After the baby was delivered, the breast mass grew in size and became painful. Courtney called Dr. Moise but the schedule was full so she was seen by Dr. Paula Pilgrim on Valentine's Day, 2005. Dr. Pilgrim examined the breast and ordered a mammogram and ultrasound. A 4-centimeter mass was confirmed.

A breast biopsy showed the mass was a breast carcinoma. Further work-up with a PET scan and a CT scan showed metastatic lesions in the liver. After several rounds of chemotherapy, a lumpectomy was done.

In an effort to control the metastatic disease, a hysterectomy and radiation therapy were done.

The Hill's filed a malpractice suit. Dr. Moise defends by claiming that the standard of care was met by her physical exam of the breast. She claims that the mass in 2005 was not the same mass that Courtney originally complained of. She also claims that even if there was a cancer in 2003, it had already metastasized to the liver.

After a jury trial, the verdict was for the plaintiff for a total of $23.6 million. Courtney has subsequently died.

Sometimes, it may be prudent to settle the case. You never know what a jury will do. If you do decide to fight the allegations, learn what you're up against. Learn as much of the law as you can to help level the playing field with your adversaries. There are defense strategies that you need to keep in mind.

Learn as much of the law as you can
to help level the playing field with your adversaries.

Statute of Limitations

In Tennessee, the Statute of Limitations for a medical malpractice case is one year from the time of the alleged wrongful act. The time starts to run when the cause of action accrues—normally this is at the time of the injury whether or not the plaintiff knows that the injury was caused by medical negligence.

The Statute of Limitations may be tolled ("tolled" is a legal term meaning that the clock stops) during the time that the plaintiff is a minor or is mentally incompetent. It may also be tolled if the defendant fraudulently conceals facts so that the plaintiff does not know that he has a cause of action.

Statute of Repose

The Statute of Repose for medical malpractice is three years in Tennessee. This starts at the time of the alleged wrongful act. This statute is different from the Statute of Limitations; if it expires, it is not possible to file a suit even if the injury occurs after that time. The purpose of the Statute of Repose is to eliminate the possibility of a claim which could arise years after the alleged act of malpractice for which maintaining records and insurance is thought to be to too great a burden and thus, unfair.

An example of this limitation would be a patient who gets an infection in a graft five years after the graft is implanted. A suit for malpractice, even if it is alleged that the infection started at the time of the operation, would not be allowed.

Service

"Service" is when the defendant is given the papers which inform him that he is being sued. If the plaintiff does not successfully serve the defendant, he will lose his case. Service is effective upon personal service of the health care provider or upon personal service of "an identified individual whose job function includes receptionist for deliveries… at the provider's current practice location."

Service is also considered effective upon mailing notice to the provider by a method described by statute.

You should keep the envelope of the letter used to prove service. The date on the postmark could be proof that the plaintiff did not make the Statute of Limitations or Repose.

Mailing in compliance with the statute will extend the statute of limitations and repose. It doesn't matter when the letter is received. The letter should go to the provider's current business address and the address listed on the Tennessee Department of Health Web site. The letter should be mailed by certified mail with return receipt requested. There should also be a Certificate of Mailing from the United States Post Office to prove that it was mailed. Of course, each state will have its own set of rules.

If the letter comes back undelivered, the plaintiff must make one more effort to give notice to the provider; however, the statute of limitations was extended with the first mailing. This last chance letter needs to go to the office where the provider last attended the plaintiff; there will be the same requirements of proof.

Standard of Care Issues

The most compelling type of malpractice case is the failure to rule out a life-threatening condition that results in the death of the patient. Myocardial infarctions, aortic dissections, cancer, and neurologic injuries represent these types of cases.

If the provider can show that he considered these types of conditions and he took the steps needed to make the diagnosis he will likely win even if the diagnosis is missed. There are false positives and false negatives for all diagnostic tests and the courts recognize this. Of course, expert testimony will be needed to confirm that the practitioner did what a reasonable practitioner would do if faced with the same or similar circumstances.

Physicians are forced to make judgments, some of which do not work out well for the patient. These decisions are made with data available; they cannot rule out every single diagnosis that might be a possibility. The juries and the courts have the benefit of 20/20 hindsight but they generally recognize this.

Plaintiff's experts also have the benefit of 20/20 hindsight but they must testify as to what they based their opinion upon. They must limit their basis on what the practitioner (defendant) had at the time he made his decisions.

The "standard of care" is defined by statute in most states. In Tennessee, it is "the recognized standard of professional practice in the profession and the specialty thereof, if any, that the defendant practices in the community in which the defendant practices or in a similar community at the time of the alleged injury or wrongful act occurred."

By law, paradigms are not the standard of care; they are not mentioned in the statute. They are only recommendations for the ideal patient who presents with a particular condition. It is rare for the patient in question to be ideal; they usually come with several unique confounders, thus the knowledge, education, training, experience, and skill of the physician must come into play.

In Tennessee, the standard of care also has a locality rule. The law will judge a physician's performance by the medical standards of the community in which he is practicing. The locality rule was originally designed to protect rural doctors who lacked the resources found in the bigger medical centers. It's not that doctors in smaller communities are trying to perform at a lower level, but the environments are different from one another and the courts recognize this.

Some states have a more restrictive community standard than Tennessee. While similar communities are allowed for the plaintiff expert to opine on the standard for the community in Tennessee, some states, like New York and Idaho, limit the standard to the community where the alleged malpractice occurred. With these restrictions, it may be very difficult for the plaintiff to find an expert in a small town willing to testify against a colleague. Without this expert testimony, his case is lost before it even gets started.

To satisfy the locality rule, the expert must relate the basis for his community standard knowledge. He will need to note similarities such as population, hospitals, medical schools, location, teaching hospitals, levels of trauma care, specialties represented, and colleges. Familiarity of the procedure in question is not enough to satisfy the locality rule.

In *Nabors v. Adams* filed in Memphis in 2009, the Plaintiff's expert (from Atlanta, Georgia), failed to satisfy the locality rule. He testified that he knew how to do a labiaplasty and it did not matter what community it was done in. He was removed as an expert, but, on appeal, a supplemental affidavit describing the communities' similarities was deemed to be sufficient to send the case back for a trial.

Medical Expert Witness

Expert testimony comes in under Rule 702 of the Tennessee Rules of Evidence. "If scientific, technical, or other specialized knowledge will assist the trier of fact to understand the evidence or to determine a fact in issue, a witness qualified as an expert by knowledge, skill, experience, training or education, may testify thereto in the form of an opinion or otherwise." The jury has the job of determining the credibility of the expert witness as is the case for every witness.

The medical expert must be licensed to practice in the state or a contiguous state a profession or specialty which would make the person's expert testimony relevant to the issues in the case and must have practiced the profession or specialty in one of those states during the year preceding the date of the alleged injury or wrongful act. These requirements apply to both the Plaintiff's and the Defendant's expert witnesses.[37]

A judge must make a preliminary assessment of the proffered expert testimony. Has the theory or technique been tested? Has it been subjected to peer review and published in a respected professional journal? Is there a known complication rate? Has it attracted widespread acceptance in the relevant scientific community?

The inquiry by the judge is flexible and focuses on the principles and methodology used by the expert. The conclusions drawn by the expert will be judged by the jury; they are not part of the judge's evaluation. Cross examination by the opposing attorney, contrary evidence, jury instructions on the burden of proof and other legal issues, are the appropriate means to challenge the conclusion of the expert.

In Tennessee, the expert must come from Tennessee or a contiguous state.[38] This requirement may be waived if the court determines that the appropriate witness otherwise would not be available.

Since medical malpractice cases are often a battle between medical expert witnesses, discrediting an opposing expert is a critical strategy in a medical malpractice action.

...discrediting an opposing expert is a critical strategy in a medical malpractice action.

Miscellaneous Strategies to Help Your Case

If a surgeon operates based on a false positive test, he will likely be removed from a malpractice case so long as his actions were reasonable. The claim would best be made against the lab that did the test. However, the surgeon might be liable if he could have done further tests to confirm the diagnosis and he did not. Plaintiff's experts may argue that a reasonable surgeon would have ordered other tests and this could be enough to bring the issue to the jury.

If the patient suffered an injury from a known risk of a procedure, then it is unlikely that a malpractice action will be brought. However, if the provider did not inform the patient of the risk, then an action may be brought based on lack of informed consent.

Documenting the informed consent process, the risks discussed, the hoped for benefits of the proposed procedure, alternative treatment along with their risks, and the risks of no further therapy, will go a long way toward the provider winning on an informed consent cause of action.

If a physician gives an order to be called for the results of a test, his failure to check back himself may be a breach of the standard of care. A practice should be in place where significant changes in the patient's status will be called to members of the team taking care him. Notifying the physician on call will probably be sufficient.

When giving orders over the telephone, spell out any drug names and have the nurse read it back. Be sure the purpose, brand, and generic are communicated clearly. Some hospitals choose to not allow telephone orders.

When storing drugs, place alerts on look-alikes and sound-alikes. Do not store drugs alphabetically and do not store confusing drugs together. Report drug names or packages that could lead to an error.

Be sure you know the patient's allergies. Know when a drug is contraindicated or may adversely react with another drug the patient is on.

Warn your patient of possible side effects. In *Burroughs v. Magee,* the plaintiff sued when her husband was killed and she was injured by a driver who was under the influence of two drugs which impaired his ability to drive.[39] The drugs were Soma, a muscle relaxant, and Esgic-Plus, a barbiturate.

Dr. Magee, the defendant, said he warned the patient of possible side effects, but he did not document this warning in the medical records. The court held that Dr. Magee had a duty to warn the patient, but no duty to warn others when he made his prescription decisions.

Testifying Under Oath? Beware and Behave!

> *Attorney:* Doctor, before you performed the autopsy, did you check for a pulse?
>
> *Witness:* No.
>
> *Attorney:* Did you check for a blood pressure?

Witness: No.

Attorney: Did you check for breathing?

Witness: No.

Attorney: So then, is it possible that the patient was alive when you began the autopsy?

Witness: No.

Attorney: How can you be so sure, Doctor?

Witness: Because his brain was sitting on my desk in a jar.

Attorney: But could the patient still have been alive, nevertheless?

Witness: It is possible that he could have been alive and practicing law somewhere.

~ Courtroom exchange between an attorney and a witness, as reported in the *Massachusetts Bar Association Lawyers' Journal* [40]

Pre-trial Testimony: The Deposition

During a physician's career, it is likely that he will be named in a malpractice action. Before the trial, any party in the action is allowed to take sworn testimony of any witness, opposing party, or any expert expected to testify at trial for the opposition. The witness will be placed under oath to tell the truth and then the lawyers from each party will be allowed, in turn, to ask questions. This pre-trial testimony is called a **deposition.**

The conduct of a deposition is very structured; the lawyers know the rules but the physicians, and other witnesses generally do not. Being forced to answer questions by an adversarial attorney while you are under oath can be stressful. It can be especially unnerving to be limited to only answering "yes" or "no" when you really have more to say, but you must play by the rules of the court. Although stressful, knowledge about the proceeding and awareness of trial strategy can make it tolerable and perhaps, allow you to perform with more confidence.

As a discovery tool, the deposition is useful to gain information that may not be in the medical records, obtain useful admissions from the witness, and box the witness in as to what he can say at the trial. It is common for the attorney to close his questioning by asking the witness if there are any other issues he will testify to at trial. If the witness says "no," then he will not be allowed to bring up new issues at the trial unless the opposing attorney "opens the door" to new testimony by asking a question that is beyond the scope of what was asked at the deposition.

There is no judge present at the deposition so any objections to a question will have to be ruled on at a later time. What usually happens is the objecting attorney will place the objection with a short legal reason which should give the questioning attorney a clue as to how to correct the question so that it will no longer be objectionable. Usually the asking attorney will change the question to pass muster, but he does not have to. The witness must answer the question unless his attorney claims the answer is protected under some privilege e.g., attorney-client or husband-wife. If the judge later sustains the objection, the answer given will not be allowed to be used at the trial.

If an attorney makes an objection to a question, he may only make it as to the form of the question; he may not make a "speaking" objection as that would give the witness a clue as to how his lawyer would like it to be answered. For example, the objecting attorney may tell the witness to answer only if he remembers or if he knows. This type of objection would never be allowed at trial so it is not allowed at a deposition, either. In fact, there are rules that make speaking objections subject to sanctions. Under the Federal Rules of Civil Procedure, the Federal Rule 30(d)(2) states, "[t]he court may impose an appropriate sanction—including reasonable expenses and attorney's fees incurred by any party—on a person who impedes, delays, or frustrates the fair examination of the deponent."

The questions and answers at the deposition will be recorded by a court reporter and the transcript of the proceeding will be given to either party provided they pay the fee for the transcript. Some depositions are video-recorded. This video may be used at trial if, for some reason, the witness is not able to attend. This video would be more effective than just having someone get on the stand and read the answers to the jury. The jury will be able to evaluate the witness's demeanor, the tone of voice, and the timing of the answers so as to get a better feel as to credibility.

Depositions are a great opportunity for an attorney to learn about the adversary's case and get a feel for the performance and credibility of the witness. Although a majority of medical malpractice cases get resolved before they ever get to trial, it is rare for the resolution to occur before the depositions of the plaintiff, defendant, and plaintiff's expert. If the plaintiff's expert isn't knowledgeable and credible, it is unlikely that plaintiff's attorney will take the case to trial; he may try instead, to push for a settlement.

There is a great deal of strategy that goes into taking depositions. Many experienced lawyers will try to get right to the heart of the matter and ask as few questions as possible to get the information they need to support their theory of the case. This "short and sweet" approach is possibly due to the fact that the witness, if it is an expert for the opposition, must be paid by the deposing attorney's side. Also, many attorneys are busy and don't want to waste time by eliciting unhelpful testimony.

Some attorneys have a different strategy. They will drag a deposition on for hours in hopes of tiring the witness out. They will then try to trap the witness into saying something harmful to the case which he would never say if he was not worn out and "un-alert."

If you are the one being deposed, your behavior is very important. You must do your best to answer the questions honestly. Do not interrupt the deposing attorney until he has finished asking the question and then wait a few seconds to give your attorney a chance to object if he needs to. Even if your attorney objects to a question, you must answer to the best of your ability unless a privilege is invoked; if this happens, your attorney will instruct you to not answer and he will let the deposing attorney know the grounds on which he is objecting. They may argue a bit and they may even have to get the judge on the phone for a ruling. Your job is to sit tight and watch the drama unfold in front of you.

In general, the deponent is not allowed to confer with his attorney during the course of the deposition. This rule has gotten some criticism as a denial of the right to counsel especially if there is a prolonged break in the questioning. Because of this criticism, most courts agree that you, as deponent, and your counsel can confer during a recess, but there should be no coaching as to how to answer the questions. Once back on the record, do not be surprised if the questioning attorney asks you what you and your attorney discussed during the break. He is allowed to ask these questions to see if any improper coaching occurred; you must answer the questions, so it is best not to put your attorney into a bind by asking him for help during the break. Once you are on the stand, as in court, you are on your own until the attorneys have finished with you.

Always be professional. You're a medical practitioner; use a professional demeanor. Be polite. A deposition is stressful but it is best to maintain your cool and answer to the best of your ability. The jury knows that you are stressed and they will respect you more if they see you are being polite—even to your adversary. Dress appropriately, too.

If you are asked a question and you don't remember the answer, it is acceptable to say that you "don't remember" or "don't recall." It is the rare individual who can recall what he was thinking at a particular time many years ago. It is not a good idea to guess at what you could have been thinking. The opposing attorney may ask you to look at the medical records and then ask if you can come up with the answer. If the chart review does not help you remember then say so.

The opposing attorney may present you with a hypothetical patient who is similar to the plaintiff and then ask for your opinions as to diagnosis and treatment. As a physician, it is fair for you to point out that the presence of the patient (one that you can actually talk to and examine) is critical to making a diagnosis and formulating a treatment plan. It is fair to be reluctant to give a definitive answer based on limited knowledge.

If your case involves a missed diagnosis which led to harm to the patient, some attorneys will persist in trying to get you to admit to a mistake. They will do this by posing a theoretical question dealing with the signs and symptoms of the patient and ask you to provide a differential diagnosis. For example, let's say the patient had an aortic dissection and the diagnosis was not made until the patient was already dead. The attorney might ask for a differential diagnosis for a patient who presents with substernal chest pain, shortness of breath, and tachycardia.

Faced with this scenario, the inclination is to say, "It could be an aortic dissection." This is especially true in light of the fact that you already know that is what the patient had. It would be truthful and better for your case if you don't jump ahead. Provide the attorney with a list of conditions that meet the proposed criteria so that the jury can actually see that the case is not as simple as the plaintiff is trying to portray. In this example, the list could include myocardial infarction, pulmonary embolus, aortic dissection, pneumonia, pancreatitis, a duodenal or gastric ulcer with perforation, costochondritis, and perhaps a sternal or rib fracture. There are other possible diagnoses you could add, but you get my point.

Remember to only answer the question that you have been asked. Many defendants feel that giving a long, detailed explanation that goes beyond the scope of the question will educate the attorney as to your thought process and make him realize that you are a knowledgeable, reasonable, and prudent physician. This is unlikely to happen and you may even be hurting your case. Actually, the more information that you provide to the plaintiff's attorney will just provide him with more material with which to ask you questions.

So if you are asked a "yes" or "no" question, you do not need to provide any explanations. For example, if you are asked if you remember seeing the patient on a particular day when there is no note by you or your team and you really do not remember, then "no" is the answer. If you say, "No, but it could have been one or two times and I just didn't document it," you will be opening yourself up to another line of questioning dealing with your documentation habits.

In a deposition, the intent of your attorney may not be to educate the jury. He may prefer to wait for the trial to do that. He may advise you to use medical terms in your answer so as to force the deposing attorney to look to you for help. This may not be the best strategy especially if your testimony ends up being read back at trial, but you will need to follow your attorney's advice. I prefer to answer in a way that would be understandable to a lay person. If your deposition testimony is being read to the jury at the trial, they may not appreciate it if they think you are talking down to them.

Do not try to be funny or sarcastic with the opposing attorney. Every word you say is being recorded by the reporter and it may not sound very good if the transcript is read back to a jury at trial.

All of the advice that I have provided for deposition behavior also applies to in court testimony. The jury and the judge will be watching your body language and listening to your tone of voice. Use this knowledge to your advantage.

It is unlikely that a clever response on your part will end up in the next edition of *Foolish Words*.[40]

New Requirements in the Tennessee Medical Malpractice Statutes

In Tennessee, medical malpractice reform was enacted in an effort to curb the filing of frivolous malpractice claims.[41] The new law put a limit on pain and suffering as has been done in several other states, but this limit has not yet been tested in court as to its constitutionality.

Now a pre-suit requirement is in place whereby a written notice of the claim must be given to each provider against whom the claim is being asserted. This notice must be given at least 60 days before the claim is filed. If the claim is filed, the pleadings must state that the pre-suit notice requirement has been met.

If the plaintiff sends a pre-suit notice, he may extend the statute of limitations up to 120 days. The 120 days runs from the day the statute of limitations or repose would have otherwise expired. However, the notice will not resurrect a claim already barred by the statute of limitations or repose.

In Tennessee, all parties are entitled to obtain a complete set of the medical records from any other party. These materials need to be sent within 30 days of receiving a written request for their production.

Another requirement is for the plaintiff to file a certificate of good faith with the court within 90 days after filing the complaint for medical malpractice. The plaintiff must confirm that he consulted with one or more experts who have provided a signed, written statement that the expert is competent to testify and he believes there is a good faith basis for filing the suit.[42]

The plaintiff does not need to disclose who the good faith expert is. The law is not clear as to who would qualify as this type of expert. Can a generalist be a good faith expert in a case against a subspecialty surgeon?

The malpractice action will be subject, upon motion, to dismissal with prejudice if the certificate is not filed.[43] The new malpractice law seems to have caused a decrease in the number of malpractice suits filed in the state since it went into effect.

Concluding Thoughts

If you are served for a malpractice suit, note the date and time you were served. Keep the envelope as it will be evidence based on the postmark. Notify your malpractice carrier immediately. They only have a limited time to respond to the allegations and they will need this time to prepare. Ignoring the case will not make it go away.

Do not alter any medical records. Plaintiff's probably already have a copy of the medical records so any additions or deletions will be noted and will reflect poorly on your credibility.

Help your lawyer understand the medical aspects of the case. This will take time but is important for you to win the case on its merits.

Stay involved. Review all of the records and read all of the testimony. This testimony includes deposition transcripts, affidavits, and Rule 26 disclosures. Help your lawyer pick appropriate experts for your side.

There is no one who knows the medical aspects of your case better than you. You are the one who took the history, examined the patient, and went over the data prior to making your clinical decisions. If your clinical decisions were reasonable, you will likely win your case.

Learn the rules of the legal arena that you are entering. The lawyers are in their comfort zone so the more you learn the better off you will be.

Never lose your cool; be polite and respect the court. The jury and the court know that you are in a stressful situation; the better you act, the more they will respect you. You are a professional medical practitioner; be sure you act like one.

> If you are sued for medical malpractice, help your lawyer understand the medical aspects of the case.
> Stay involved. There is no one who knows the medical aspects of your case better than you.
> You are the one who took the history, examined the patient, and went over the data prior to making your clinical decisions. If your clinical decisions were reasonable, you will likely win your case.
> Learn the rules of the legal arena that you are entering.
> Be polite and respect the court.
> You are a professional medical practitioner; be sure you act like one.

Talk #7:
Themes for Malpractice Defense

Review, Recall, and Action

Citations

[37] Tennessee Rules of Evidence Rule 702.
[38]Contiguous states are the states bordering Tennessee. These states are Mississippi, Alabama, Arkansas, Georgia, Kentucky, Missouri, North Carolina, and Virginia.
[39] 118 S.W.3d, 323 (Tenn. 2003).
[40] Ward, Laura: **Foolish Words, The most stupid words ever spoken,** PRC Publishing Limited, New York, 2003,
p. 120.
[41]TCA section 29-26-121.
[42] Good faith means "more probable than not."
[43] A dismissal with prejudice means the plaintiff cannot refile the lawsuit even if he corrects the problem.

Talk #8: Health Care Talking Points

$

Both Republicans and Democrats agree that health care costs are too high and that there are too many people that are not covered by health care insurance. The goals of health care plans from these two main political parties are remarkably similar; it's the methods of meeting those goals that are in contention. I believe that for a health care plan to work, it must lead to (1) a decrease in costs, (2) access to health insurance for everyone, (3) patient choice in tailoring their plans and shopping for care, (4) emphasis on preventative care, and (5) some form of tort reform.

It is estimated that health care constitutes one-sixth of the American economy and is growing. The Affordable Care Act (ACA) was passed, in part, to reign in those costs. Prior to passage of the ACA, there were 34 million people without health care insurance. The new law was structured to get these people insured.

How did health care become so expensive? It probably dates back to World War II when President Roosevelt placed controls on wages and prices to help finance the war effort. Companies started to offer health benefits to attract workers. These benefits were not reported to the IRS as income. Subsequently, the IRS ruled that health benefits paid by employers would be tax exempt; this ruling conceded that the health care system would now involve third party payers.

Medicare took root in the early 1960s as part of President Johnson's Great Society. This was based on a fee-for-service model and costs took off. Not too surprising if we assume that people act rationally.

Is the premise that health care costs are rising really true? This is hard to say. In 1989, Americans spent 5.1% of household expenditures on health care. In 1999 they spent 5.3% and in 2003, they spent 5.9%. In 2008, the percent of household spending was pretty much the same. It seems that the percent of what we spend is pretty stable. Maybe it's okay to spend 6% of our costs on health care. Of course spending as a dollar amount is increasing, but it's increasing for everything as our population grows and our wealth increases.

Despite the high costs of health care, arguments are put forth that state that the health care provided in America suffers in comparison to other developed countries. For example, there is data that Americans have a lower life expectancy, higher infant mortality rate, and lower overall health performance. Is it really that bad in the United States?

Life expectancy in America was 77.9 years in 2007 and this was below several western nations. However, there are several factors other than health care that were not considered in this analysis. There are higher levels of homicide and auto accidents in America. There are 14.2 auto deaths per 100,000 population compared to 9.25 in Canada, 7.4 in France, and 6.2 in Germany. If we take out homicides and car accidents, then we have the highest life expectancy of western nations.

International comparisons of health care can be misleading in other areas also. Infant mortality rates are higher in America but we count every birth where the baby shows any signs of life. This follows the World Health Organization definition of a live birth where the baby, once removed from the mother, "breathes or shows any other evidence of life such as beating of the heart, pulsation of the umbilical cord, or definite movement of the voluntary muscles."[44]

In Europe, babies born before 26 weeks of gestation are not considered to be "live births."[45] In Switzerland, a baby must be 30 centimeters long at birth to be considered alive. France requires a medical certificate stating that the baby was born alive and viable to be counted. In Canada, high risk pregnancies are sent to the United States for delivery.

The Patient Protection and Affordable Care Act

The Patient Protection and Affordable Care Act (ACA) was signed into law on March 10, 2010. It is over 2,400 pages long and it is difficult to read; I tried. It will likely add $1 trillion to our health care costs over the next ten years.

The Act will force businesses to provide health insurance for their workers or be fined if they do not. The uninsured will be forced to buy health insurance or be fined if they do not. There will be attempts to lower costs yet provide care to an additional 34 million people. I believe the lower costs will be borne by the health care providers who will be paid less, much less.

The Act calls for an additional 159 new boards and commissions such as an Elder Justice Council, Pregnancy Assistance Fund, and Office of Indian Men's Health. Lobbyists favorable to the Democratic Party were well rewarded.

Under the ACA, "comparative effectiveness research" will be done to decide what care will be allowed. This clause is probably where the "death panels" claim originates.

There will be new bureaucracies to ensure compliance with the law, monitor insurance companies, and penalize taxpayers who don't buy health insurance. It is estimated that the law will add 16,000 new IRS agents to find those who don't purchase health insurance and to help collect the new taxes that are part of the bill.

During the health care debates, Nancy Pelosi (D California) claimed that the ACA would save taxpayers $1.3 trillion. Ezekiel Emanuel, one of the bill's architects, projected savings of $1 trillion. Showing lack of agreement even among the bill's advocates, the Obama administration predicted that the new law would actually increase costs. The Congressional Budget Office (CBO) claimed that deficit reduction would be unlikely with the new law.

Making predictions of future health care costs is difficult. In 1965, Medicare costs were projected to be $9 billion in

1990. The actual costs were $67 billion. The actual costs in 2010 were projected to be $521 billion but this included the added prescription drug benefit.

There are many reasons for faulty cost projections. One is that they do not take into account that people act in a rational way; they will likely demand more goods or services if they don't have to pay for these out of their own pocket. Another reason for error is for the assumptions not to pan out. Medicare reimbursements were supposed to go down 23% for surgeons but Congress has kept pushing this cut into the future.

Good Ideas in the ACA

Several good ideas are imbedded in the Affordable Care Act. For example, pre-existing conditions can no longer be used to deny a person health care coverage. This provision was immediately put into effect for children and goes into effect for adults in 2014 assuming the President does not make a change.

Small businesses (composed of less than 50 employees) will get tax credits of up to 50% of employee premiums.

The "donut hole" which limits prescription medication expenditures over $2,700 will be decreased by 50%.

The cut off age for young adults to be covered by their parent's insurance rises to 27.

Lifetime caps on health insurance expenditures will be eliminated.

Adults with pre-existing conditions will initially be covered in a high risk pool; all adults, even those with pre-existing conditions, will be covered in 2014.

All insurance plans must include preventative care without co-pays by 2018.

Insurance companies will no longer be able to cut someone from coverage if they get sick and start to require payments for on-going health care.

The new law now requires more transparency from the insurance companies. Insurers must reveal how much they spend on overhead. This clause was included based on the presumption that insurance companies were spending a great deal on overhead and not enough on medical services. Since there was already data from Centers for Medicare and Medicaid Services (CMS) that about 86% of premiums were being spent on health care, it is uncertain that there will be much gain with this requirement.

Any new plan under the ACA must implement an appeals process for coverage determinations on claims. It should make it easier for the insured to get redress for claims that are denied or inadequately funded.

There will be a 10% tax on indoor tanning services. It's doubtful that this will raise much money for the ACA, but it may lead to a decrease in skin cancers over the long term.

Because of the perception of fraud and abuse, the ACA provides for more screening to try and eliminate this waste. Tying insurance and billing to the Internal Revenue Service, programs can be written to uncover potential fraud and allow for more scrutiny of the individuals involved.

Of course, it is the government that will define fraud and abuse so there is potential for conflict. Even if the provider is correct in the care provided, he may have to spend money for the high cost of defending his actions. This could lead to similar situations that occurred in the Physicians at Teaching Hospitals (PATH) audits, where teaching hospitals were pressured to settle rather than face the potential for catastrophic financial losses.

Medicare will be expanded to rural areas.

Third party payers will be required to maintain a medical loss ratio (income/outgo) of 85% or higher to take advantage of IRS tax benefits. This clause is intended to keep premiums lower but will put the insurance companies at risk of loss if their projected payouts exceed what is predicted in their mathematical models.

In hopes of getting the public to eat more responsibly, restaurants will be forced to disclose the nutrient content alongside their menu items.

In an effort to reduce the high cost of coverage, temporary programs will be created to allow companies to provide early retiree health benefits for those in the 55-65 age range.

Money will be set aside in the ACA to allow for better consumer information on the Internet so that patients can be better able study health insurance options. Unfortunately, they will still not be able to cross state lines to buy insurance policies as there is no provision in the law to allow this.

The plan allows for a two year credit of up to $1 billion to encourage investment in new therapies for the prevention and treatment of disease but it is not specified as to how this money will be allocated. Will it be spent thru the National Institutes of Health or some other federal agency?

Maybe the High Cost of Health Care Is Worth It

Mary Lasker has said, "if you think that research is expensive, try disease."[46]

Maybe the cost of our health care is high because it is the best in the world. Many of our treatments actually work. Cancer treatments, HIV treatment, cardiac and vascular surgery advances are generally felt to be the best in the world. Vice President Dick Cheney had a left ventricular assist device keeping him alive for quite a while until he received a heart transplant. When the Russian president, Boris Yeltsin, needed heart surgery, the Russian government sent for Dr. DeBakey's team from Baylor. It is not unusual for other world leaders to send their families or themselves to our country for their own health care.

Maybe we should be looking for other ways to decrease costs instead of "dumbing down" what is arguably the best health care system in the world. Since the fee for service model got us into this mess, perhaps we need to go back to a free market system for health care and limit the government to providing a safety net for any catastrophic illness.

Other Ideas that Might Work

Several other ideas have been discussed to help make health care costs affordable. For example, vouchers of $5,000 for the purchase of health insurance with tax-free dollars would allow people to shop for policies that meet their budget and their needs. This would not require a large bureaucracy; it would only require people to process the forms and police the system for fraud. This would allow for the people to have a vested interest in their health care policy, and the free market should decrease these costs.

Updating Medicare by allowing each senior $250,000 to purchase elder care insurance would allow seniors and their caregivers to shop for their own medical care. This should decrease costs as this population would be empowered to look for the best deals.

Health care providers would be encouraged to provide charitable care if this care would be tax deductible. This would make it easier to treat low income and uninsured patients. Another benefit of this change would be to free up emergency rooms to take care of emergency cases; this would be cheaper than having the uninsured rely on the ER for their primary care.

Tort Reform

If we are truly interested in decreasing health care costs, something will need to be done regarding tort reform. Malpractice insurance is costly. For some specialties, premiums can be over $200,000 per year and these costs are transferred to the patients. Defensive medicine as a strategy to defend against potential malpractice claims raises the cost of health care for everyone.

Estimated costs for defensive medicine are about $124 billion per year and rising.

Some states limit the payment for non-economic damages in a malpractice suit in an effort to control malpractice premiums. Some states may soon try to take malpractice claims out of the hands of juries with alternative forms of resolution such as Health Courts.

Limiting attorney's fees is another strategy being looked at to decrease the costs of malpractice premiums. Decreasing premiums may decrease charges for patients but more will need to be done.

Mandates in Health Insurance Plans

The ACA mandates benefits that must be included in health care plans. This raises costs as people are forced to pay for benefits they will never use. These mandated "benefits" raise the price of policies by about 10%. For other forms of insurance, people are allowed to pay for the coverage they want and can have the deductibles that they want. That's how insurance is supposed to work.

By eliminating community rating (where everyone is charged the same amount) premiums would come down for most people.

People should not have to pay for plans mandating care for in-vitro fertilization, cosmetic surgery, and abortions. The ACA requires coverage so that premiums will be higher so that money will be available to pay for plans that will use the mandated benefits. We are all paying for benefits that only a few will use. Health care political pandering if you will.

People should be allowed to pay for the coverage they want and obtain the deductibles that they want.
That's how insurance is supposed to work.
We are all paying for benefits that only a few will use.
Health care political pandering if you will.

Buying Insurance across State Lines

People should be able to cross state lines to buy health insurance. State regulations create large cost disparities. For example, a 25-year old male, non-smoker in Newark, New Jersey, pays $3,263 for a Preferred Provider Organization (PPO) while in Louisville, Kentucky, the same coverage can be purchased for $336. These State regulations prevent the Newark person from buying the Kentucky policy. This effectively protects the New Jersey underwriters from outside competition. This is a clear violation of the free market which works best if we can buy what we want and are free to cross state lines to get the best deals.

Health Savings Accounts

One way to cut health care costs is to put people back in charge of their own routine care. The best proposal to do this is to let people set up health savings accounts where tax free dollars will be used to pay for routine care. Medical providers will be forced to compete for these dollars by offering the best services for the lowest price.

Once the free market is back in play, drug companies, hospitals, and doctors will not be able to raise prices without losing patients.

The health savings accounts could not be used for over-the-counter remedies and penalties would be imposed for those patients who make non-medical withdrawals.

Once the free market is back in play,
drug companies, hospitals, and doctors
will not be able to raise prices without losing patients.

Taxes and Insurance Premiums

Premiums for health insurance should be deductible from taxes; if companies can do it (and they can) then individuals should be allowed to do it also. This would allow most of the 176 million enrolled in company owned health plans to buy their own insurance and force the companies to compete by offering supplemental tax free compensation to allow the consumer to buy more insurance if they see the need. This would be especially valuable for the employee with a pre-existing condition.

Portability of Health Insurance Plans

Health coverage should be portable. Employees should be able to control their own health plans and should be able to take these plans with them from job to job. This would force employers to treat their workers better since they would not be locked into a job for fear of losing their health care insurance.

Health insurance should be like other insurance, i.e., auto, life, home, and fire. The plans would be private property and they would allow for maximum choice. They should be flexible and creative allowing the consumer to pay for a policy they deem necessary to meet their needs. This would remove big business, labor unions, and politicians from the health insurance business and let the free market control the costs.

The Public Health Service Clause

Due to rising costs of doing business and decreasing reimbursements, many health care providers are opting for early retirement. However, the Public Health Service Clause which is buried in the ACA may give the government the power to draft physicians as the need arises and place them in areas of the country where the government determines they are needed. It used to be that physicians were subject to a draft in times of war and the draft was for military service. This is a new far-reaching power in the ACA. It is surprising how little press has been given to this new governmental power over physicians. Physicians cannot retire if the government needs them.

Conclusion

None of the ideas that I have mentioned in this article will lead to a decrease in the quality of care. I believe in American exceptionalism and I believe that the American people will not stand by and let the quality of care go down. Unfortunately, the ACA will lead to a decrease in quality as it must rein in costs. If nothing else, rationing of health care is built into the law to keep costs from rising.

My Grandparents used to say that you should pay for the best doctors if you are sick and pay for the best lawyers if you have a legal problem. You're looking for the best return on your investment and there is nothing more important than your health. It is said that there are problems that money can solve and then there are *real* problems. Perhaps we are spending more on health care because we are getting better health care.

None of the ideas that I have mentioned in this article will lead to a decrease in the quality of care.
I believe in American exceptionalism and I believe that the American people will not stand by and let the quality of care go down.
Perhaps we are spending more on health care because we are getting better health care.

The debate on health care in America is on-going and highly contentious. It is wise for all health care providers to keep up on this issue as it is likely to affect more than just their incomes.

Talk #8: Health Care Talking Points

Review, Recall, and Action

Citations

[44] Geneva Foundation for Medical Education and Research.
[45] Bernadine Healy, "Behind the Baby Count," US News and World Report, September 24, 2006
[46] The Lasker Award, often a precursor for the Nobel Prize in Medicine, was named after her.

Talk #9:
Regulation of Provider Conduct: Medicare and Medicaid

From the website: "CMS covers 100 million people......through Medicare, Medicaid, the Children's Health Insurance Program, and the Health Insurance Marketplace. But coverage isn't our only goal. To achieve a high quality health care system, we also aim for better care at lower costs and improved health. But, we can't and we don't, do it alone. We need your help to find the way forward to a better health care system for all Americans."

Americans spent nearly $1.9 trillion on health care goods and services in 2004. This was 16% of the Gross Domestic Product (GDP). This was a per capita rate of $6,280. These costs are projected to reach $4 trillion in 2015. This would be about 20% of the GDP. This cost is not sustainable. Medicare is projected to be $800 billion in 2015; this would be about 56% of federal health care outlays.

Medicare Part A covers the in-patient hospitalization costs and includes prescription medications that are given in the hospital. Medicare Part B covers the payments for the physicians' services and some of the outpatient services not covered under Part A. Medicare is financed by payroll taxes and monthly premiums for voluntary supplemental coverage.

Medicare and Medicaid were enacted in 1965 and it was a "pay for procedure" model. When the law was passed, there was only one provision which prohibited making false statements in the billing process. Today, there are numerous health care related criminal, civil, and administrative anti-fraud laws and regulations, both state and federal.

"Fraud" is the knowing misrepresentation of the truth or concealment of a material fact to induce another to act to his or her detriment. Fraud is usually a tort, but in some cases, especially when the conduct is willful, it may be a crime.

How common is fraud and abuse in the health care billing arena? We really do not know. However, it is generally said to be about 10% of the costs. This 10% number is really a political statistic; it was not derived by any empirical data. The Government Accounting Office came up with the number based on an unscientific survey of unidentified individuals who were asked to estimate losses from fraud and abuse. We don't know who these people were and we don't know how they came up with this number.

Enforcement of the federal criminal laws relating to health care billing fraud is the responsibility of the Department of Justice. The Federal Bureau of Investigation has the responsibility to investigate possible health law violations.

Administrative enforcement of health care laws is the responsibility of the Department of Health and Human

Services. The HHS Office of the Inspector General investigates and enforces any administrative sanctions.

The states have their own sets of laws dealing with health care fraud. These laws deal with Medicare and Medicaid fraud (remember the states are the ones paying the bills up front; they expect to be reimbursed by the Federal government), illegal kick-backs, self-referrals, etc. Local prosecutors can bring their own cases and this is a good way for them to make a name for themselves if they are interested in a political career.

Private parties can also bring civil lawsuits; however, the government has the option to take over the suits if they feel such action is warranted.

Prosecutors have much discretion. They can choose which laws and which punishments to pursue. The prosecutor may have his own political or personal agenda and he may choose accordingly.

Criminal statutes dealing with health care fraud include:

1. Conspiracy to defraud the United States—18 USC section 286, 371
2. False statements—18 USC section 101
3. Mail fraud—18 USC section 1341
4. Wire fraud—18 USC section 1343
5. Money laundering—18 USC section 1956, 1957.

Other Health care specific statutes are:

1. Kickbacks—42 USC section 1320(a)-7b(b)
2. Health Care Fraud—18 USC section 1347
3. Theft or embezzlement—18 USC section 669

4. False statements—18 USC 1035 and 42 USC sections 1320a-7b(a)
5. Obstruction—18 USC section 1518
6. Money laundering—18 USC section 1956(a)(1).

Several statutes have been written to regulate provider conduct to help control the costs of health care. These include the following:

1. False Claims Act
2. Stark 1 and 2
3. Medicare/Medicaid Fraud and Abuse Statute
4. State laws criminalizing referral fees
5. State medical practice acts.

False Claims Act

Of all the possible laws applicable to Health Care fraud, the False Claims Act has the biggest financial bite. This law was enacted in 1863 in response to rampant fraud being perpetrated on the Union army during the Civil War. Over 140 years, multiple amendments have expanded this law to encompass virtually any entity that transacts business with the federal government.

Commercial transactions used to function with a "Buyer Beware!" attitude where the burden was placed on the buyer to be sure he was getting what he was paying for. If the Army was buying 1,000 horses but only 800 were healthy, then the Army, the buyer, absorbed the loss. Having suffered several such losses, the government said enough of that nonsense, so they wrote new laws.

Under the False Claims Act, violators are liable for civil penalties of $5,500 to $11,000 per claim, plus 3 times governmental damages. These penalties can be astronomical and will often lead to settlements before being brought to court. For example, if someone were being charged with 100 false claims, then they would be at risk of a $1.1 million fine regardless of the value of the false claim.

Under the law, sampling errors can be extrapolated to the total number of bills. If a hospital sends out 1,000 bills a week and the auditor finds a 10% error in the billings, then that can be about 5,000 errors in a year. At $11,000 per error, then the liability could be $55 million for the year. Since it would be more realistic for a hospital to have over 1,000 bills a day, we are looking at about a $400 million dollar fine in a year. Not many hospitals could afford that kind of financial hit.

A physician was accused of receiving an overpayment of $245,392. Every bill he submitted subsequent to this collection was considered fraudulent because there was a billing requirement he had not committed any previous fraud. He was sued for a penalty of $81 million. The District Court imposed a substantially lower sanction, but the risk of a catastrophic financial loss was significant.[47]

In *United States v. Pani,* the government sued a neurosurgeon who submitted 157 claims for surgeries he did not perform. Pani lost under the civil False Claims Act and under associated criminal charges.[48]

Anti-Kickback Statutes

No kickbacks are allowed under Medicare or Medicaid. Any fines and penalties are put back into the Medicare Part A trust fund.

Stark

Under Stark laws, it is illegal to have a self-referral arrangement in which physicians are rewarded for sending or keeping business in institutions they own, contract with, or are employed by. Fee-splitting is not allowed. These laws were meant to curb increased utilization of health care services.

The penalties under Stark were primarily civil, not criminal. There was strict liability whereby "intent" is not an element of the violation. This strict liability removed legal uncertainty—all financial relationships are in its scope and then the exceptions are spelled out. (See **Talk #3: Stark Reality** for further information on this complex set of laws, page 45.)

Although there are no criminal penalties under Stark, many states have their own medical practice acts which do have criminal penalties for self-referrals. This means that jail time could result for violators.

There are other state medical practice acts which may even lead to disciplinary action such as revocation or suspension of a physician's license to practice.

Can a heart surgeon send a percent of his surgical fee to the referring cardiologist? Of course not. What if he buys the cardiologist a nice gift for Christmas? If the prosecutor sees this as a form of kick-back, a prosecution may result.

The best way to stay out of trouble is to avoid any semblance of a "kick-back" for referring a patient to another entity.

State Licensing Boards

It is common for state licensing boards to have their own regulations. Failure to meet requirements may lead to loss of a license to practice as well as other administrative, civil, and criminal penalties. Check with your state to see what your risks are.

State licensing boards may also have ethical precepts; these do not have the force of law but they do require practitioners to act in their patient's best interests.

Qui Tam Suit

Qui Tam suits allow for whistle-blowers to sue on the government's behalf. They can retain 15%—30% of the proceeds of the suit. This provides a powerful incentive for policing in the health care market. Disgruntled employees, competitors, patients, and their families may all sue under the Qui Tam statutes.

Grounds for a Qui Tam suit include mischarges—billing for services not delivered, false negotiations, and fraud-in-the-inducement whereby all claims filed under a contract are false, and false certification—where certification is a prerequisite to obtaining a government benefit.

Other grounds for a Qui Tam suit include claims for substandard products and services. Also, reverse false claims, where the defendant uses a false record to decrease or avoid a financial obligation he owes the government, can be a cause of action. In the traditional false claims action, the government is only entitled to recover the difference between what it paid to the defendant and what it should have paid given the defendant's misrepresentations. By tying this to the False Claims Act, much higher recoveries may be had.

Misrepresentation

In *United States v. Lorenzo,* a dentist fraudulently billed routine dental checkups which were not covered under Medicare, as "consultations" for oral cancer which were billable.[49] This is a misrepresentation to get paid for services that Medicare did not intend to cover; i.e., routine dental care. The government was awarded over $18 million based on 3,683 false claims.

It is also illegal to misrepresent the identity of the person who furnishes the services. This occurs when the original provider is not eligible for reimbursement but the name of another provider is used so that billing would be allowed. In *Peterson v. Weinberger,* a physical therapy company billed in the name of an independent physician who did not perform the services.[50] This is misrepresentation and led to a financial penalty of over $100,000 and loss of the ability of the physician to participate in Medicare.

If a provider renders a legitimate service but bills for a more expensive category of care, this is "upcoding" and is not allowed. In *United States v. Krizek,* a psychiatrist billed for 45 to 50 minute sessions when he only spent 20 to 30 minutes with each patient.[51] In fact, the court found that the billings on some days approached 24 hours. The Krizeks were found liable for monetary damages and they were enjoined from participating from Medicare and Medicaid until they could show the Court that they could abide by the relevant rules for billing.

Standard of Care Issues

Occasionally, the government has brought suit based on standard of care issues, but these are hard to prove because they are fact intensive. The government can only review the medical records and they don't have the clinical knowledge of the provider that was actually taking care of the patient, so in these types of cases the defendant is likely to win—if they choose to fight. However, since the risk of losing the case is high, a settlement may be the only reasonable option.

There are other examples where the government has used the False Claims Act, with its high cost of claims, to push providers to settle. The Academic Medical Centers were faced with these types of claims with the PATH audits.[52]

PATH Audits

In June 1996, the Office of the Inspector General (OIG) initiated a plan to audit teaching hospitals. The OIG wrote, "This initiative grows out of the extensive work performed by the OIG at a major East Coast University. The focus of the review was compliance with intermediary Letter 372 (IL-372), the Medicare rule affecting payment for physician services provided by residents. We found that the institution was not complying with this rule. We also found that the teaching physicians were improperly 'upcoding' the level of service provided in order to maximize Medicare reimbursement."[53] This audit initiative was predicated on the belief that attending surgeons were billing for services that were being done by residents with little or no attending supervision. The inspectors focused on the medical records looking specifically at the documentation of attending supervision. The rule that was put in place required documentation of supervision and if that documentation was inadequate, then services could not be billed for.

The University of Pennsylvania was found to be billing despite "inadequate documentation." There were 1.4 million claims submitted during the audit period. The hospital for the University of Pennsylvania calculated that even if only 2% of the records had inadequate documentation, they would be at risk for statutory penalties of $280 million under the False Claims Act (not including treble damages for overpayments). The hospital concluded that settling was the only viable option. A $30 million settlement was paid.

PATH audits were taking off. The OIG was likely to get lucrative settlements without ever having to go to court. All teaching hospitals and medical schools were at risk.

The University of Washington agreed to a $35 million settlement after a neurosurgeon tried to suborn perjury by having his residents say he was in the operating room when he generated bills. As I've said before, always tell the truth, especially when you're under oath. You do not want to go to jail and lose your license to practice medicine.

Dartmouth Hitchcock Medical Center was found to have only a minimal billing error ($778) after an extensive PATH audit. However, Dartmouth's bills for defending the audit totaled $1.7 million. Costs were high even with a victory.

The OIG originally planned to audit all teaching hospitals, but lobbying efforts led to Congressional hearings. The hearings led to a moratorium on the PATH audits, but this moratorium could end at any time. In the meantime, the teaching hospitals have worked hard to come into compliance for documentation of resident supervision at all levels.

Other Examples of Fraud

An Illinois radiology center allowed physicians to lease their MRI and CT scanners for a fee of $400. The physicians would then charge the patient's insurance companies up to

$800 for the scans. The physician would pocket $400 for doing nothing except referring the patient. This scheme was discovered and the radiology group had to pay a $1.2 million settlement and they had to agree to stop paying illegal kickbacks to referring physicians.

A University contracted out for cardiovascular services with a "for profit" private practice group in town. The group got the Medicare A dollars paid for resident supervision. In turn, the group paid the University Practice Plan 10% of their net collections. It was this "send back" that made the scheme illegal.

A trauma service participating in a research protocol was paid $10,000 for every patient enrolled in a drug study. Some of this money was earmarked for tests that were needed for the study. Unfortunately, the hospital billed the patient's insurance coverage for these same tests. This double dipping was fraud.

Whenever a lot of money is moving back and forth and it's hard to define what is what, this sets up a situation for a money laundering prosecution; this is where illegal gains are disguised as legitimate dollars. The circumstances can be complex which puts the prosecutors at a distinct advantage.

Summary

False Claim Act violations, upcoding errors, wire fraud, mail fraud, racketeering, anti-kickback laws, Stark violations and Health Insurance Portability and Accountability Act

(HIPAA) violations are just a few of the many laws in place to keep health care providers from committing fraud in the delivery of health care. It seems like physicians and other providers are at an unfair disadvantage. Too bad. That's just another price of doing business as a provider.

What should a provider do to protect himself? First, he should be aware of the law and he should do his best to follow it. It is important to read Medicare/Medicaid carrier advisories and manuals. Records should be clear and they should **never** be destroyed. All contracts should be reviewed by legal counsel. Every practice should have a compliance program in place and all employees should be educated as to the requirements of the program.

If a provider can show that he was trying to do the right thing, the prosecutor may decide to leave him alone and go after the worst offenders. This "prosecutorial discretion" can work to the provider's advantage.

What should a provider do to protect himself?
First, he should be aware of the law
and he should do his best to follow it.

Talk #9:
Regulation of Provider Conduct: Medicare and Medicaid

Review, Recall, and Action

Citations

[47] *United States v. Krizek,* 111 F.3d 934 (D.C. Cir. 1997).
[48] *United States v. Pani,* 717 F.Supp 1013 (S.D.N.Y. 1989).
[49] *United States v. Lorenzo,* 768 F.Supp 1127 (E.D. Pa 1991).
[50] *Peterson v. Weinberger,* 508 F.2d 45 (5th Cir. 1975).
[51] *United States v. Krizek,* 111 F.3d 934 (D.C. Cir. 1997).
[52] PATH is the acronym for Physicians At Teaching Hospitals
[53] Ruth SoRelle, Tracking a Tangled PATH, **Circulation,** 1998; 97: 2191.

Talk #10: Morbidity and Mortality Conference – What Is Protected? What Is Discoverable?

"All relevant evidence is admissible except when it isn't."

As a surgeon, it is important to learn from your mistakes. It is even better to learn from someone else's mistakes. It is not unusual for a case that is discussed at a Morbidity and Mortality (M&M) Conference to later be the subject of a malpractice action. It could be very damaging for the minutes of the morbidity and mortality conference to be discoverable since many of the admissions or recommendations would be favorable to the plaintiff.

Are the proceedings of the M&M conference privileged? After all, it is in the public's interest for the discussions to be frank so that future care could be improved. Discussions are unlikely to be open and critical if there is a fear that the records of the meeting could be used by the plaintiff's attorney in a malpractice action.

The State of Tennessee does recognize a Medical Review Committee—informant Privilege in *TCA section 63-6-219(e).*

This law states that the records of that committee "…shall be privileged communications subject to the laws pertaining to attorney—client privilege." However, before a law is truly understood, case law needs to be developed to see how the courts interpret it. Sometimes the court's opinion can be difficult to figure out and, in fact, different judges may have different opinions as to what the law means.

Lawyers are trained to argue on either side of an issue; their stance is really the stance of the client. The lawyer will look for case law that supports his client's position but he must also present contrary case law to the court if it is from a "controlling legal authority." This means that he must educate the court as to the law of that jurisdiction. If the case law is contrary to his client's position, the lawyer will do his best to show that the facts of the case are different from the underpinning facts of the contrary case law.

As a surgeon, it is important to learn from your mistakes. It is even better to learn from someone else's mistakes.

In *Weekoty v. United States,* Mr. Weekoty died while under the care of a Unites States Health Service physician. The case was discussed at the M&M conference of that hospital. The plaintiff sued and the Magistrate granted a motion to compel presentation of documents that were related to the M&M conference. On appeal, the appellate court reverses. "The material sought by Plaintiff's Motion to Compel is protected by the self-critical analysis privilege, perhaps more properly called the medical peer review privilege, and is not subject to discovery or introduction at trial."[54]

Not all courts recognize the peer review privilege of the M&M conference. In *Syposs v. United States,* the plaintiff subpoenas "peer review" records as to procedures undertaken by Dr. Lorenzo Teruel. The court held that these records must be presented to the plaintiff as the court did not recognize a medical peer review privilege.[55] This court reasoned that the hospital failed to "provide any reason to believe some physicians would not provide candid appraisals of their peers absent the asserted privilege." In fact, "Congress in providing protection for those involved in peer review did not establish a privilege for most documents created in the process."

The *Syposs* court felt that the protections in the law were for the participants in the peer review process; these participants were protected from a defamation lawsuit. The protections were not for the practitioner who may be later named in a malpractice action. In effect, immunity from suit is not immunity from disclosure. The public's need to know relevant facts in a federal litigation outweighed the defendant's peer review privilege.

In *Syposs,* "[This] court finds an absence of objective experience supporting the view that strict confidentiality of peer reviews is an essential prerequisite to achieving the public's interest in maintaining quality health care."

Attorneys rarely think of the beauty of the law or its rational development. They are primarily concerned with the needs of their clients and how the law can best be applied (or changed) to accomplish those goals. If they want to access your privileged information, they will do everything in their power to get it.

Federal Rule of Civil Procedure 26(b)(5) states that a party objecting to a discovery request must identify and describe the privileged information and materials being withheld without revealing the underlying protected information. For an M&M conference it would be appropriate to acknowledge that the case in question was discussed at the conference, but the comments, opinions, and minutes generated at the meeting would be privileged. This acknowledgment would meet the intent of the Rule without revealing any privileged information.

In all jurisdictions, a party seeking discovery may bring a motion seeking an order to disclose the information claimed to be privileged. This motion will force the Court to decide on a case by case basis if the privilege will be recognized.

Even if the privilege is recognized by the Court, the people identified as participating in the conference may still have to testify as to the facts of the case. Facts are always discoverable. A person cannot be allowed to hide facts under the umbrella of a privileged communication.

Facts are always discoverable.
A person cannot be allowed to hide facts
under the umbrella of a privileged communication.

Attorneys rarely think of the beauty of the law or its rational development. They are primarily concerned with the needs of their clients and how the law can best be applied (or changed) to accomplish those goals. If they want to access your privileged information, they will do everything in their power to get it.

Unintentional Waiver of the Privilege

Even if the Court recognizes a peer review privilege, a party can waive the privilege by knowingly and voluntarily disclosing information. For example, a defendant may testify that "the M&M conference acknowledged that I was not negligent." By this testimony, the door is opened for a cross examination of all that went on at the M&M conference. As an aside, only the trier of fact can determine the issue of negligence so the defendant's testimony is pretty irrelevant on this issue.

It is also possible to lose the privilege via an unintentional waiver. This could happen if the privileged material is sent out to opposing counsel as a result of a mistake. If this happens, the courts have different ways of handling it.

Some courts hold that the privilege is "never waived." This approach means that inadvertent disclosure can never constitute a waiver because there was no subjective intent to disclose the information.

Other courts have a "strict accountability" approach which holds that an inadvertent waiver is a fully effective waiver of the privilege. This approach is harsh; it encourages the clients and lawyers to be ever careful and vigilant, or else.

Many courts use a "balancing of the circumstances" test which looks at (1) precautions taken, (2) time it took for the disclosing party to recognize the error, (3) the scope of the production, (4) the extent of the disclosure, and (5) the overriding interest of fairness and justice.

Your attorney will advise you of what your court does if you are faced with this situation.

Medical Review Committee Privilege

At least 46 states have statutes that protect the work of medical review committees. These statutes protect the committee members from liability and they protect the proceedings (records, materials produced, materials considered). Information that is otherwise discoverable is not protected just because it was brought up at the committee meeting. The goal of the privilege is to ensure open discussion during the meeting so that meaningful improvements in medical care can be realized.

Many states have codified the rules in such a way as to permit parties who were present at a medical review committee meeting to testify at a deposition or trial, but allowing them to not testify as to information obtained as a result of the meeting itself.

If the privileged information is disclosed to a third party, such as a government regulator, it is not clear that it can be kept from opposing parties who are seeking that information in the course of litigation. The case law pertaining to the Securities and Exchange Commission is clear that the information is waived. The case law is divided as to whether other privileged information is impliedly waived with the disclosure. So, for example, if you report the failure of a medical device to the Food and Drug Administration, and that information came out at the M&M conference, other information that you think is privileged may not be any more.

Evidence

All relevant evidence is admissible except when it isn't. There are several rules which may not allow relevant evidence to be admissible; such as if there is a privilege attached to the evidence. Relevant evidence is "evidence having any tendency to make the existence of any fact that is of consequence to the determination of the action more probable or less probable than it would be without the evidence." [56] Clearly, M&M findings are relevant, especially if one of the parties admits culpability. On the other hand, evidence that is not relevant is not admissible.

If a party admits he screwed up during the M&M proceedings, this would be a party opponent admission and this would be admissible evidence if it were not protected under the Peer-review privilege.

If the M&M conference makes recommendations so that the particular complication would be minimized in the future, that evidence would not be admissible to prove strict liability, negligence, or culpable conduct in connection with the event.[57] However, if these recommendations are released, then all of the protections of the conference would likely be lost.

The evidence of subsequent remedial measures could also be used to impeach a witness who claims, "there was nothing else he could have done to prevent the complication." It would be best to keep anything emanating from the M&M conference confidential if at all possible.

> All relevant evidence is admissible except when it isn't…
> It would be best to keep anything emanating from the M&M conference confidential if at all possible.

Patient Safety and Quality Improvement Act of 2005

On July 29, 2005 the Patient Safety and Quality Improvement Act went into effect. The goal of the law was to have health care providers present their errors without fear of reprisal. The intent was to improve the quality of care which is an important public policy interest. The law would allow for surgeons, and others, to submit their results to a patient safety organization certified by the Department of Health and Human Services as long as patient confidentiality would be maintained. The results would then become part of a national data base of medical errors which could be analyzed so that new care systems and best practices could be developed to prevent the same types of errors in the future.

But wouldn't this reporting essentially remove the protections of the Peer-Review committee? I think it would. Releasing the information, even to a governmental body, historically, makes the information discoverable for other purposes. There is no "safe harbor" written into the law

Remember, protected information does not include information that is collected, maintained, or developed separately, or exists separately from a patient safety evaluation system. This type of information, if reported to a patient safety organization, shall not, by reason of its reporting, be considered to be a patient safety work product.

It is also true that if a patient safety organization is construed as a regulatory agency, then this information will become discoverable.

Can the M&M committee become a patient safety organization so that it will have its proceedings protected under the Act? The answer is probably yes. First, the committee would have to be certified by the Secretary of Health and Human Services. The committee would need to have policies and procedures in place that are designed to improve patient safety and the quality of health care. The committee would also need to collect and analyze a patient safety work product which would then need to be disseminated for purposes of encouraging patient safety.

As with other privileges, there are exceptions whereby the privilege will not be allowed. For example, in a criminal proceeding, if the material is not reasonably available from other sources, then the information must be revealed. This goes to the fact that a criminal defendant must have access to any information that may help prove his innocence.

How likely would it be for a medical negligence case to rise to a level of a criminal proceeding? Not too likely, but it has precedence.

Medical Negligence as Criminal?

Although medical negligence comes under the heading of torts, there are instances where the medical negligence was deemed to be so egregious, the District Attorney assigned to the jurisdiction decided to press criminal charges.

An eight year old boy died during a routine ear operation. The anesthesiologist was charged with manslaughter and criminally negligent homicide. He was found innocent but he did lose his license.[58]

A surgeon in New York was found guilty of second degree murder after he performed a second trimester abortion and the patient bled to death from a lacerated cervix.[59]

The case against Rosalyn Scott was especially chilling for surgeons. In this case, a Los Angeles County sheriff was shot multiple times. He was taken to a Level 1 trauma center at Drew University. He underwent a nine hour operation and then went to the Intensive Care Unit (ICU) where Dr. Scott, the Vice Chair of Surgery, was consulted. She was not the operating surgeon. After 36 hours in the ICU, the sheriff died.

An anonymous complaint was made to the District Attorney's office and he decided to investigate the case against Dr. Scott as a homicide instead of just a malpractice claim. Of course the claim against the shooter was also for homicide, but the claimed "gross negligence"[60] and "reckless disregard"[61] alleged against Dr. Scott could also have been criminal and contributing to the death.

The Grand Jury refused to hand down an indictment so the District Attorney recommended that the licensing board revoke Dr. Scott's license, which they did.

There was uproar in the medical community. Several independent reviews of the case concluded that the Medical Board's charge of "gross negligence" was unfounded. It took two years for the Board to rescind the charges.[62]

Other Times When the Privilege May Not Be Allowed

The owner of the privilege always has the option of voluntarily disclosing the information. Also, the Secretary may disclose the information if he deems it consistent with the goals of the Act.

During a whistle-blower action where the provider of the information has suffered an adverse employment action such as a loss of employment, failure to get a promotion, or failure to attain any other employment benefit for which the individual would otherwise be eligible, then the information would be discoverable. This goes to the fact that a Civil Rights action takes priority over the Peer Review privilege.

Conclusion

If the surgical M&M conference is to have the privileges of a peer-review committee, it would be wise to have the Department of Surgery apply for certification as a Patient Safety Organization with the Secretary of Health and Human Services. It would be important to recognize the faculty and the surgical residents as "qualified" staff and have no students or visitors to the M&M conference.

The findings of the M&M conference should be disseminated to the surgical community at regular stated intervals and these findings should be used to encourage a culture of patient safety and to help find ways to minimize future patient surgical risk.

A viable alternative would be to have the American College of Surgeons serve as a Patient Safety Organization thru which, the findings of various M&M committees could be funneled and then disseminated to all surgeons. This alternative would fail if the College of Surgeons were subsequently found to be a "regulatory body."

It has been said that at M&M conferences, the ABC's of surgical case defense are: Accuse, Blame, and Criticize.[63]

Surgical education would be adversely affected if these conferences could not be held in confidence. When doctors disagree, it would be a step backwards to let the jury decide who is correct.

When doctors disagree, it would be a step backwards to let the jury decide who is correct.

Talk #10: Morbidity and Mortality Conference – What Is Protected? What Is Discoverable?

Review, Recall, and Action

Citations

[54] *Weekoty v. United States,* 30 R.Supp.2d 1343 (D.N.M. 1998).
[55] *Syposs v. United States,* 63 F.Supp.2d 301 (W.D.N.Y. 1999).
[56] Tennessee Rules of Evidence, Rule 401.
[57] Tennessee Rules of Evidence, Rule 407. This rule deals with subsequent remedial measures.
[58] USA Today, October 19, 1998, Section D, 1-2.
[59] New York Times, September 13, 1995, Section B, 3.
[60] Gross negligence is defined as "a conscious, voluntary act or omission in reckless disregard of a legal duty and of the consequences to another party."
[61] "Reckless disregard" means "a conscious indifference to the consequences (of an act)."
[62] *LA CMA Physician*, September 1997, 29-34.
[63] *A Surgeon's Little Instruction Book.*

Talk #11:
The Medical Expert Witness

In order to win a malpractice case, the burden is on the plaintiff to prove, by a preponderance of evidence standard, that the defendant (1) owed the plaintiff a legal duty, (2) the defendant, by acting negligently, breached that duty, (3) the plaintiff suffered actual damage, and (4) it was the defendant's negligence that was the proximate, or legal cause, of this damage. If evidence of all these elements is presented, then a prima facie case for negligence has been shown.[64]

The Burden of Proof

For a medical malpractice action in Tennessee, the jury shall be instructed that the claimant has the burden of proving, by a preponderance of the evidence, the negligence of the defendant. The injury alone does not raise a presumption of the defendant's negligence. The plaintiff must prove the recognized standard of acceptable professional practice in the profession and the specialty thereof… in the community… or in a similar community at the time the alleged injury or wrongful act occurred. Plaintiff must also prove that the defendant acted with less than, or failed to act with, ordinary and reasonable care in accordance with such standard.

The plaintiff must also prove that as a proximate (legal) result of the defendant's negligent act or omission, the plaintiff suffered injuries which would not otherwise have occurred. This is the causation issue.

It is usually uncontested that the defendant owed a duty to the plaintiff; the defendant, a health care provider, owes a duty to act within the standard of care for his patients. The other elements need to be proven with expert testimony since "standard of care" and "proximate cause" issues are beyond the usual knowledge base of the average juror. Since expert testimony is required, an "expert" will need to testify. So what constitutes an "expert?"

The qualifications necessary to be a medical expert witness are spelled out in Rule 702 of the Federal Rules of Evidence. According to the Rule, the expert can be qualified by "knowledge, skill, experience, training or education." Whether a witness qualifies as an expert can only be determined by comparing the area in which the witness has superior knowledge, skill, experience, or education with the subject matter of the witness's testimony.

The American College of Surgeons has other requirements beyond that called for by the Rules. The College states that the expert must have a current, valid, and unrestricted license to practice medicine in the state in which he or she practices and he should be a diplomat of a specialty board recognized by the American Board of Medical Specialties. The specialty should be appropriate to the subject matter of the case in question.

> ...the expert can be qualified by "knowledge, skill, experience, training or education."
> Whether a witness qualifies as an expert can only be determined by comparing the area in which the witness has superior knowledge, skill, experience, or education with the subject matter of the witness's testimony.

The College also states that the expert should be familiar with the standard of care at the time of the alleged occurrence and he should be actively involved in the clinical practice of the specialty during the time that the testimony is provided. The expert should also provide evidence of continuing medical education relevant to that specialty.

The College requires the expert to document the percentage of time he is involved as an expert witness and he should disclose the amount of compensation he obtains from such activities.

The College of Surgeons also has guidelines as to behavior of the expert witness during the process. The College requires the expert to review the medical information in the case and testify to its content fairly, honestly, and in a balanced manner. The opinions that the expert proffers must be based on the facts of the case and he must distinguish between actual negligence (sub-standard medical care that results in harm to the patient) and an unfortunate medical outcome such as a recognized complication of the treatment.

The expert should review the standards of practice prevailing at the time of the alleged occurrence and he should state the basis of his testimony or opinion and be prepared to discuss alternate methods and views during his testimony.

The expert must state what his compensation for testifying is and this compensation should be reasonable. The compensation may *not* be contingent on the outcome of the case.

The opinions that the expert proffers must be based on the facts of the case… the expert is ethically and legally obligated to tell the truth.

As with any witness, the expert is ethically and legally obligated to tell the truth. Failure to provide truthful testimony exposes the medical expert to criminal prosecution for perjury, civil suits for negligence, and revocation or suspension of his or her professional license.

"The impact of expert witnesses on modern-day litigation cannot be overstated; yet, to some, they are nothing more than willing musical instruments upon which manipulative counsel can play whatever tune desired."[65]

"Expert witnesses testify regarding subjects outside the common knowledge of the finder of fact, so the jury cannot rely on the experience and common sense of its members to ferret out distorted evidence."[66] As such, it is effective cross examination that will test the validity of the expert's testimony. In fact, it is Federal Rules of Civil Procedure number 26 (and the associated state rules which mirror this federal rule), which ensures that full and effective cross examination of an expert witness could be done by opposing counsel.

A Case on Point

A 60-year old man had a persistent pneumonia for about a year. Antibiotic therapy controlled the pneumonia but it would always recur when the antibiotics were stopped. He was sent for an open lung biopsy which revealed adenocarcinoma of the lung with metastatic disease to the pleura. His thoracotomy wound became infected so the skin edges were opened and dressing changes were done until the infection cleared. The wound was then closed at the bedside a week later.

The patient had a difficult year with worsening pulmonary status until he finally died. The family brought a malpractice suit against the thoracic surgeon alleging pain and suffering and wrongful death all due to the post-operative wound infection. They ignored the fact that he had metastatic lung cancer.

The plaintiffs could not find a physician medical expert but they did find a nurse who was an infection control specialist. This nurse was willing to testify as to standard of care issues relating to the thoracic surgeon. After seven years of discovery, the case was finally dismissed as the court did not feel the nurse was acceptable to comment on standard of care and causation issues as they pertain to a thoracic surgeon. After all, she was not a thoracic surgeon nor had she ever participated in a chest operation.

Bias of the Medical Expert

The medical expert must be prepared to state the basis of his opinions. Since the lawyer working with the expert "can all too easily color the expert's opinion by simply controlling the expert's access to information," it is only with effective cross-examination that this potential for bias can be uncovered.[67]

There is no expert-attorney privilege unless the defendant is also functioning as an expert. This means that in most cases, the opposing side will be able to access these communications which may be used to show the influence that the lawyer has achieved over the expert's testimony. This can be used to impeach the expert.[68]

"[Counsel]...may push the expert's testimony from the realm of sloppy science into that of biased science."[69]

Remember, the expert is not allowed to be paid on a contingent basis. He may not claim a percentage of the winnings. Also, if the expert's fees are so high as to seem unfair, the jury may decide that he is being paid to testify in a manner leading to bias in favor of the side he is testifying for. The opposing attorney should be able to bring out these facts with an effective cross-examination.

The Locality Rule

The state of Tennessee also has a locality requirement for an expert witness. This requirement is for the expert to be licensed to practice in the state or a contiguous bordering state in a profession or specialty which would make the person's expert testimony relevant to the issues in the case, and had practiced this profession or specialty in one of these states during the year preceding the date of the alleged injury or wrongful act. This rule applies to expert witnesses for both the plaintiffs and defendants.

In Tennessee, the court may waive the locality rule if it determines that the appropriate witnesses would not otherwise be available. This waiver probably could not occur unless there is a hearing on the issue and the court is convinced that the witness in contention has some knowledge, experience, or skill that would not be found in the state or contiguous states but would be relevant to the case. However, the waiver provision will also be applied in a situation where the plaintiff is unable, after exercising reasonable diligence, to obtain expert witnesses to testify in her favor except by going outside of Tennessee or the contiguous states.[70]

In *Rose v. HCA Health Services of Tennessee,* the affidavits pertaining to the locality knowledge of the proffered expert witness were "generalized and unspecific, and reflected only a cursory effort to find an appropriate expert from Tennessee or a contiguous state."[71] This court concluded that the trial court was correct in not waiving the locality rule.

In *Ralph v. Nagy,* this court did not waive the locality rule as to two New York physicians since the plaintiff admitted that he had other *appropriate* witnesses on the issue of causation.[72]

"Before going to war,
learn all you can about your enemy."
~ Sun Tzu — *The Art of War*

Talk #11: The Medical Expert Witness

Review, Recall, and Action

Citations

[64] Prima facie is a legal term meaning that the plaintiff has produced "enough evidence to allow the trier-of-fact to infer the fact at issue and rule in the plaintiff's favor." **Black's Law Dictionary**

[65]John Langbein, 52 U. Chi. L. Rev. 823, 835 (1985).

[66] Lee Mickus, 27 Creighton L. Rev. 773, 787-788 (1994).

[67] Id.

[68] Id.

[69] Id.

[70] *Crumley v. Memorial Hospital,* 509 F. Supp.531, aff'd, 647 F. Supp. 164.

[71] *Rose v. HCA Health* ***Services*** *of Tennessee,* 947 S.W.2d, 144.

[72] *Ralph v. Nagy,* 749 F. Supp. 164.

Talk #12: The Federal Tort Claims Act and the National Practitioner Data Bank

Many physicians and other health care professionals have chosen to work for the federal government in the Veterans Administration, the Department of Defense, the Public Health Service, or other federal health care systems. One of the key benefits of working in these systems is that the United States will be responsible for any torts of the employee so long as the employee was performing within the scope of his duties.

The Federal Tort Claims Act (FTCA) was passed by the United States Congress in 1946. The intent of the Act was to reduce the negative impacts of Doctrine of Sovereign Immunity whereby the government was immune from suit. With the Doctrine, Congressmen would introduce bills to help their constituents who had been injured by the negligence of governmental employees. These individual bills would allow the injured party some redress. The Congress recognized that these bills were an inefficient method for dealing with these claims so they wrote a new law.

With the Federal Tort Claims Act, the United States government gives its consent to be sued in Federal Court in front of a district court judge without a jury. The laws used would be the laws of the place where the act or omission took place.

There are numerous exceptions where sovereign immunity still applies such as the Post Office losing letters, the government enforcing unconstitutional statutes, actions of the military in the time of war, damages caused by fiscal operations of the Treasury Department, intentional torts, etc.

Under the FTCA, the Federal Courts have jurisdiction for "torts by government employees acting within the scope of their duties."[73] The claim must be brought against the United States of America. The health care practitioner does not need to have malpractice insurance since he is covered by the United States; all judgments will be paid by the United States.

Contractors are not considered "government employees," so health care providers working under a contract will need to have their own malpractice insurance since the United States will not pay for judgments against them.

The process for dealing with a medical malpractice claim under the FTCA is very different from that used in the various State courts. First, the claim must be filed within two years of the incident or knowledge of the incident should have reasonably been obtained. This may be different from the Statute of Limitations for the particular State.

Once the claim is filed, the plaintiff may not file a suit with the Court for six months while the government decides whether to allow or deny the claim. If the case has not been resolved during the six month review period, the claimant may then file a suit. He has six months from the date of the denial to file.

A settlement or judgment paid on a malpractice claim may subject the health care practitioners involved in the case to reporting to the National Practitioner Data Bank (NPDB) and to State licensing boards. These reports can impact negatively on the practitioner's ability to maintain his credentials and privileges at the place where he practices and his ability to seek work at another location.

A surgeon applied for privileges at a Veterans Administration Medical Center (VAMC) but he had several listings on the NPDB. He was allowed to withdraw his application because a denial of privileges would have triggered another report to the NPDB.

The National Practitioner Data Bank

In 1986, the Health Care Quality Improvement Act went into effect. A section of this law established the National Practitioner Data Bank. Congress was under the impression that the quality of medical care in the United States was decreasing and was becoming a nationwide problem. Congress believed that physicians were being discouraged from participating in meaningful peer review and, as a result, substandard doctors were being allowed to practice without fear of oversight.

Any adverse action taken against a physician was not available to an outside reviewer. As a result, physicians could go to another practice location, usually another state, and get a new license and start a new practice without having to account for his previous record.

The intent of the NPDB was to restrict the ability of incompetent practitioners from moving from state to state without disclosing their previous malpractice payments and any other adverse actions e.g., licensure, privileges, and professional society memberships. The NPDB was a clearinghouse to collect and release information that was believed to be related to professional competence and conduct. This data would be available to entities involved in granting (or denying) credentials and privileges to physicians and to the licensing boards for the various states.

The Bank would function as an alert system. The information it contained was limited, but it was intended to lead to further inquiry into a practitioner's licensure, malpractice history, behavior, and professional society memberships. The burden was still on the hospitals, licensing boards, and other health care entities to make final hiring, credentialing, and licensure decisions.

More on the Federal Tort Claims Act (FTCA)

Under the FTCA, the government will not be liable for any interest prior to judgment or for punitive damages. That's the law.

Any person who alleges that an employee of the federal government has caused an injury must commence the lawsuit only under the Federal Tort Claims Act (FTCA). Some plaintiff's attorneys ignore this requirement and will contact the practitioner directly in hopes of inducing a settlement—this action may be a violation of the Rules of Professional Responsibility but the plaintiff may be willing to take this risk.

For alleged malpractice, the requirements on the plaintiff are the same in the Federal system as they are in State courts. The plaintiff must prove by a "preponderance of the evidence" that they were injured by the negligent acts, or failure to act, of the health care practitioner. Punitive damages are not allowed under the FTCA—even though state law may allow them. Federal law trumps the state law and this is one of the reasons that plaintiff's attorneys do not like having to use the Federal courts for a medical malpractice cause of action.

The Veterans Administration

Malpractice claims against Veterans Administration (VA) physicians and dentists are handled under the Federal Tort Claims Act. The plaintiff must first seek an administrative remedy before he can bring a suit against the United States. If a payment is made as a settlement during the administrative process, it is possible for the practitioner to be named to the National Practitioner Data Bank.

The majority of medical malpractice claims brought against the VA (United States) under the FTCA do not result in any payment as the cases are usually denied by Regional Counsel. If a payment is denied, the plaintiff then has the option of bringing suit in the Federal court system.

If a suit is filed in the Federal Court, the case will then proceed as any other malpractice action that would usually be brought in the State court system. The laws of the State would apply as there is no federal medical malpractice law.

If a payment is made to the plaintiff, the Medical Center Director where the case occurred must make a list of all the practitioners involved and then send the list to the VA Office of Medical-Legal Affairs (OMLA). The Director must also send all pertinent documents related to the claim. This reporting does not involve the Office of Regional Counsel and the practitioners on the list may not even be the providers who were originally contacted by Regional Counsel during the original investigation of the claim.

Once notified of the settlement or judgment (if the case went to court), OMLA will then form a review panel consisting of at least three health care professionals to review the case and make a judgment regarding the care that was provided by the individuals at risk of being reported to the NPDB. Each practitioner being reviewed is allowed to make a written statement concerning their role in the case. This is the practitioner's chance to convince the panel that he did not breach the standard of care (the negligence issue) and/or his actions did not lead to the harm claimed by the plaintiff (the causation issue).

The panel must include a member of the same profession and specialty as appropriate, of the practitioner who is being reviewed. Each panelist must review all materials pertinent to the care that led to the claim. The panel must then decide, by majority vote, if the care that led to the claim constituted substandard care, professional incompetence, or professional misconduct.

A health care provider may be reported to the NPDB if a settlement or judgment is paid to the plaintiff of a malpractice suit if the payment "...is related to substandard care, professional incompetence, or professional misconduct on the part of the physician, dentist, or other licensed health care practitioner."[74]

The process by which the VA decides on whether or not to make a report to the NPDB is related to a Memorandum of Understanding between the VA and the Department of Health and Human Services where it was agreed that certain malpractice payments made for the benefit of the practitioner would be submitted to the NPDB.

When the Review Panel determines that the standard of care was met and there was no professional incompetence or professional misconduct, or the injury was due to circumstances beyond the practitioner's control (power failure, drugs mislabeled by supplier, equipment malfunction, etc.) then no report will be sent to the NPDB.

Once the Director has been notified that a payment has been made, he has 30 days to notify all of the involved practitioners. The practitioners will then have the opportunity to provide a written statement concerning the care that led to the claim. The request for a statement does not imply blame or fault. This statement will be sent to the Panel for consideration. This is the one best chance for the provider to plead his case.

The written statement should focus on the care provided and should argue that the care was within the standard of care expected of a practitioner of like knowledge, experience, training, education, and skill. If applicable, he should also argue that his care was not the cause of the patient's harm. These two issues are the "standard of care" and "causation" elements of a medical malpractice case which must be proven by the plaintiff by a preponderance of the evidence standard.

The written statement is very important because the Panel is likely to give it great weight in coming to its decision.

A Case

A patient with coronary artery disease underwent a three-vessel coronary bypass. Grafts were placed to the left anterior descending, the posterior descending, and the diagonal coronary arteries. He had a small circumflex system that could not be bypassed with a graft. He developed chest pain several months after the operation and a stenosis of the right coronary graft was successfully stented. The patient brought a suit claiming that the circumflex system should have been bypassed instead of the diagonal.

A payment was paid by Regional Counsel. The defendant wrote a rebuttal letter stating that the diagonal vessel was in the intermediate distribution of the circumflex coronary, the circumflex was too small to bypass, and the culprit lesion was in the right coronary which was fixed.

The review panel report quoted freely from the rebuttal letter. This demonstrated the importance of the rebuttal letter. The facts of the case were explained and were confirmed by a review of the medical records. The panel used the letter as a guide to their review.

Remember, no one knows the case better than you. You were the one taking care of the patient and following the course. However, you may want to have a lawyer help you with the rebuttal letter as there may be issues of law that you are not comfortable with, such as standard of care and causation.

The Role of the Medical Center Director

If the Panel concludes that a report should be made to the NPDB, it is the Medical Center Director who submits this report. The Director must also notify practitioners as to the conclusions of the Panel. Appropriate State licensing boards must also be notified in accordance with the Handbook requirements.

The Medical Center Director is prohibited from entering into a formal or implied agreement to not make a report to the NPDB in return for a personnel action, e.g., resignation, retirement, or reassignment.

Who Is at Risk?

Reports must be submitted to the NPDB if a payment is made for the benefit of a licensed physician; this includes residents and interns. Payments may be made for the benefit of medical and dental students, but these will not be reported to the NPDB. Payments made for the benefit of deceased practitioners will be reported because a fraudulent practitioner could assume the identity of the dead person; this reporting would be a way to catch these individuals.

If there are multiple practitioners named in the malpractice action, the payment will be apportioned if possible. If the amount cannot be fairly apportioned, then the total amount will be reported along with the total number of practitioners on whose behalf the payment was made.

It's Not Over Until It's Over

If the practitioner believes the report to the NPDB has factual inaccuracies, he should contact the reporting body and request that a correction be filed. If the body declines to change the report, the provider is then allowed to add a statement or initiate a dispute of the report, or both, through the NPDB dispute process. This process is external to the reporting body (such as the VA) and is initiated by the practitioner through Health and Human Services.

The dispute process cannot be used to protest a payment or to appeal the underlying reasons for the reporting. It can only be used to dispute the factual accuracy of the report or claim that the report was not submitted in accordance with NPDB reporting requirements. This is a good thing to keep in mind if you were not notified in a timely fashion or were not given the appropriate documents to allow for a written rebuttal before the report was filed.

Be aware that in the Federal Tort Claims process, Regional Counsel may make a payment to the plaintiff for strategic reasons. The OMLA may decide differently, concluding that the payment was made due to a breach of the standard of care; it may then recommend that a report be filed with the NPDB.

If the provider is not diligent, this report may be filed with the NPDB without the practitioner ever exercising his right to make a written response. He should not let this happen!

Many physicians and other health care professionals
have chosen to work for the federal government
in the Veterans Administration,
the Department of Defense,
the Public Health Service,
or other federal health care systems.
One of the key benefits of working in these systems
is that the United States will be responsible
for any torts of the employee so long as the employee
was performing within the scope of his duties.

Talk #12: The Federal Tort Claims Act and the National Practitioner Data Bank

Review, Recall, and Action

Citations

[73] *United States v. Smith,* 499 U.S. 160, 166 (1991).
[74] VHA Handbook 1100.17.

Talk #13:
The Emergency Medical Treatment and Active Labor Act (EMTALA)

The first duty of society is justice.

~ Alexander Hamilton

In 1986, the United States Congress enacted the Emergency Medical Treatment and Active Labor Act (EMTALA). The intent of the act was to ensure public access to emergency services regardless of the patient's ability to pay.

The Act imposed specific obligations on Medicare participating hospitals that provide emergency room services to first provide a medical screening exam to anyone who presents to their facility for emergency care. After the medical screening exam is complete, the hospital must then provide stabilizing treatment if an emergency condition is identified. If the hospital is not capable of stabilizing the particular emergency condition, or if the patient requests to be transferred, then the hospital must arrange for an appropriate transfer to a facility that is able to manage the emergency medical condition.

A Representative Case

On November 5, 1994, 63-year-old Millard was involved in a motor vehicle accident (MVA). The Emergency Medical Technicians (EMTs) arrived at the scene at 10:28 a.m.[75] The accident scene was 14 miles from the Audrain Medical Center (AMC) and 25 miles from the University of Missouri Medical Center. Since the EMTs found no measurable blood pressure or radial pulse, they chose to transport to Audrain.

Dr. Corrado was the general surgeon on call for Audrain but he had signed out to Dr. Ben Jolly, an orthopedic surgeon, so that he could attend an American College of Surgeons local meeting. Unfortunately, Dr. Jolly did not have general surgery privileges and Dr. Corrado had not notified anyone else that he would not be available for call.

Millard arrived at AMC at 11:07 a.m. IV fluids were started and a chest radiograph was obtained. The chest film showed an increased density on the left side which was consistent with blood in the chest. The Emergency physician examined Millard and he concluded that she was also bleeding into the abdominal cavity.

Two pager communications for Dr. Corrado were not answered. At 12:00 p.m., air transport was called but they were grounded due to bad weather. At 12:07 pm, Dr. Jolly entered the ER and saw the patient. He agreed that she needed an abdominal exploration but he did not have the privileges or experience to do that operation.

At 12:23 p.m., Dr. Corrado responded to the previous pages. After being told the situation with the patient, he agreed that she should be transported to the University of Missouri Medical Center. At 1:45 p.m., the patient arrived at the University of Missouri where she underwent an abdominal exploration beginning at 2:15 p.m.; this was about four hours after the MVA.

The patient ended up losing her left kidney and gall bladder, and part of her colon and small bowel. She brought suit alleging, "as a direct and proximate result of the delay in treatment caused by Dr. Corrado's absence, (she) sustained aggravation of the injuries she sustained in the accident and additional serious injuries."[76]

Dr. Corrado filed a motion for Summary Judgment because, he argued, the plaintiff had failed to establish the formation of a physician-patient relationship—a necessary component showing that Corrado owed her a duty of care. A duty of care is a necessary element of a medical malpractice action which the patient must prove by a preponderance of the evidence standard.

The trial court agreed with Dr. Corrado. The court granted the motion and entered a judgment in favor of Dr. Corrado.

On appeal, the judgment was reversed. The appellate court held that the public policy of Missouri and the foreseeability of harm to patients in the position of the plaintiff support the recognition of a duty flowing from Dr. Corrado to Mrs. Millard. The "on-call" physician owes a duty to reasonably foreseeable emergency patients to (at least) provide notice to the hospital when they will be unavailable to respond to calls.[77]

The court went on to say that the duty to provide adequate notice will not have a detrimental impact on the ability of hospitals to attract physicians to accept "on-call" assignments. The original judgment was reversed and the case was remanded for further proceedings consistent with the opinion.[78]

A concurring opinion sums up the "duty owed" issue very well. "One who undertakes, gratuitously or for consideration, to render services to another which he should recognize as necessary for the protection of a third person or his things, is subject to liability to the third person for physical harm resulting from his failure to exercise reasonable care to protect his undertaking if his failure to exercise reasonable care increases the risk of such harm…"[79]

Since the plaintiff produced substantial evidence that Dr. Corrado's actions resulted in a delay in obtaining treatment for her injuries, thus increasing the risk of harm, then Dr. Corrado was not entitled to a summary judgment.[80]

How Courts Interpret Statutes

When courts are interpreting written statutes, the first thing they do is look at the plain language of the law. If the wording is unambiguous, then they use that language.

Unfortunately, many laws are ambiguous and are open for different interpretations. When the law is ambiguous, the courts will then study the legislative history, the debates on the issue. These debates can be used to guide the courts as to what the legislature intended the law to be.

If the legislative history is not clear, the courts will then base their decision as to what public policy mandates. The factors involved in public policy considerations are the social consensus as to the interest worth protecting, the foreseeability of harm and the degree of certainty that the protected person may suffer an injury, and the moral blame the society attaches to the pertinent conduct.

Other public policy factors that the courts will consider are the prevention of future harm, the cost of the conduct and the ability to spread the risk of loss, and the economic burden upon the actor and the community related to the conduct.

The analysis of the court in *Millard v. Corrado* concluded that Dr. Corrado did owe a duty of care to Mrs. Millard. Also, Dr. Corrado had a contractual obligation to AMC to notify them if he would not be available to cover. The court also construed a contractual obligation for the "on-call" physician to respond to being called in a reasonable time, i.e., 30 minutes.

In many hospitals, physicians are not required to take call. The duty mandated by the court for the on-call person, did not, in the court's opinion, make it too difficult for the hospitals to attract physicians to accept "on call" assignment. The physicians could charge the hospitals for being on call and they could also bill for the patients they saw while they were on call. The physicians were also rendering a service to the community which the court felt the physicians should be willing to do.

The United States Congress was to codify the law as it pertained to patients presenting to emergency rooms with the Emergency Medical Treatment and Active Labor Act in 1986.

The Emergency Medical Treatment Active Labor Act (EMTALA)

Due to a perception that several hospitals were "dumping" the indigent patient population, some of whom had unstable medical conditions, on the so called "Charity" hospitals, Congress enacted the Emergency Medical Treatment Active Labor Act.[81] Under this law, any hospital that has an Emergency Department (ED) **must** provide, for any patient that presents to the ED, an appropriate medical screening examination within the capability of the hospital's Emergency Department, including ancillary services routinely available.

If the screening examination shows that the patient has an emergency medical condition or is in active labor, the hospital must then provide, within the hospital's capability, further examination and such treatment as may be required to stabilize the medical condition, or transfer the patient to another facility which has the capability to stabilize the condition.

EMTALA also requires the hospital to maintain a list of on-call physicians who must be available to come in and help treat the patient with an emergency medical condition and that physician must be able to come to the emergency department in a reasonable amount of time. The on-call physician must not refuse to appear or he and the hospital will be subject to penalties.

A participating hospital that negligently violates a requirement of EMTALA is subject to a civil penalty of not more than $50,000.00 for each violation. An on-call physician who negligently violates a requirement of EMTALA is subject to a civil penalty of not more than $50,000.00 for each violation and, if the violation is gross and flagrant or is repeated... exclusion from participation in this subchapter (Medicare) and State health care programs.[82]

In *Burditt v. HHS* [83] a physician was fined by Health and Human Services (HHS) but damages could not be recovered from him in a private cause of action; however, a private cause of action was allowed against the offending hospital.

There are several examples of close calls for an EMTALA violation. In February 2001, the on-call surgeon was contacted to see a trauma patient with a perforated atrium. He was in the OR doing an operation at that time and he could not come. Fortunately, his partner was available and was able to fix the atrium in a timely fashion.

In April 2001, a patient presented to the emergency room with a knife wound to the chest. The on-call surgeon was out of the country (and had not checked out to the hospital or any other surgeon). Another thoracic surgeon was called who came in and did the case. These examples led to a change in the hospital policies so that the on-call physicians were forced to cover as required.

On-call physicians need to be aware that an EMTALA violation is not considered malpractice so any fines will not be covered by their malpractice carrier. Also, it is unlikely that the hospital or the department will pay for the physician's fine. The penalties will need to be paid by the physician from his own resources.

In the case of hospitals which provide services for which Medicare may pay, the hospital **must** maintain a list of physicians who are on call for duty after the initial examination to provide treatment necessary to stabilize an individual with an emergency medical condition.[84] The obligation of a physician to serve on a call schedule is legally based on state law governing contracts, derived from agreements attendant to medical staff membership, rather than an obligation on the physician by Federal law.[85]

Since contracts that require one of the parties to commit an illegal act are void, a physician who knows that he cannot meet the requirements of EMTALA cannot be made to take call. In this situation, the hospital will need to make other arrangements.

There was a University who had one cardiac surgeon who was forced to cover several hospitals including one with a Level 1 trauma center. Since that surgeon knew he could not cover every hospital and he knew that he was personally liable for any fines that could result from

EMTALA violations, he refused to take call at the trauma center. The hospital with the trauma center had several options. It could recruit for other cardiothoracic surgeons, it could remove all cardiothoracic services from the hospital in which case they could transfer these patients, or they could manipulate the call list. They chose the last option.

The call list had only a phone number for cardiothoracic emergencies. The phone number was for a lower level surgical resident who could not have "provide[d] treatment necessary to stabilize [the cardiothoracic emergency conditions]" which was required by the statute. This was a violation, but since the cardiothoracic surgeon always came in when called, there were no patients that fell through the cracks which would have triggered an investigation by the Office of the Inspector General.

In order to trigger an EMTALA investigation, a party must show that they were injured in part by a failure of the hospital to comply with the law. Since the cardiothoracic surgeon in the above example was able to come in (even though he was no longer on the call list), there were no injured parties who had standing to bring a suit. It is not advisable for any hospital to follow this example.

Enforcement

The enforcement of EMTALA is the responsibility of the Office of the Inspector General (OIG) for Health and Human Services (HHS). Regional offices of the Center for Medicare and Medicaid Services (CMS) may cite a hospital for failure to stabilize an emergency medical condition. Each year, the number of settlements for EMTALA violations has been increasing. This is likely to continue under the Affordable Care Act which has several sections looking to recoup funds for fraudulent activity on the part of providers.

> Under EMTALA, any hospital that has an
> Emergency Department (ED) **must** provide,
> for any patient that presents to the ED,
> an appropriate medical screening examination
> within the capability of the hospital's
> Emergency Department,
> including ancillary services routinely available.

The Supreme Court and EMTALA

The Supreme Court has weighed in on some of the areas of EMTALA. In *Roberts v. Galen of Virginia,* the Court ruled that there is no requirement for appropriateness in this law. The lower court had held that the appropriate medical screening duty required proof of an improper motive for the defendant to be liable. This was overruled by the Supreme Court which held that it is not necessary that proof of an improper motive be proven for recovery under the stabilization requirement.[86]

In re Baby K, parents of an anencephalic child[87] kept bringing her to the emergency room with repeated episodes of respiratory distress. The hospital asked a court for permission to not treat this child the next time she presented as the case was terminal and the care was futile. The 4th Circuit held that there is no exception for futile care under EMTALA.[88] This decision meant that the hospitals must do a screening exam and stabilizing treatment on all patients, regardless of the patient's situation. This made EMTALA more than just an anti-dumping statute. Even patients with terminal conditions now had to be examined and, if necessary, stabilizing treatment started. The Supreme Court refused to grant certiorari (a writ used by the Supreme Court to review the cases it wants to hear) so the plain language of the statute, which has no exception for futile care, must be followed.

Plaintiff's attorneys are being creative in their usage of EMTALA. They may threaten to report an EMTALA violation to either CMS or to the OIG on the theory that the hospital failed to follow their own rules which had been set up to comply with EMTALA. Some hospitals may be willing to settle a medical malpractice claim to avoid this reporting. In this respect, EMTALA is functioning as a federal malpractice act!

By using EMTALA violations as a separate theory of liability, plaintiffs then have the option for federal jurisdiction. This may constitute a strategic option due to the different rules of civil procedure and the different statutes of limitation.

Hospitals have also been creative in dealing with the requirements of EMTALA. Some jurisdictions will throw out "failure to stabilize" claims if the patient has been admitted to the hospital. In these cases, the hospital must show that there were admitting orders written for that patient.

Some hospitals show compliance by creating an "on-call" policy outlining exactly what the on-call physician must do for a patient presenting to the emergency department. The policy usually follows the requirements of the law and there must be disciplinary actions against the physician who fails to comply. These policies will shift the blame from the hospital to the provider.

Another action that hospitals have taken to get out from the under the law, is to eliminate their emergency departments altogether. This seems to go against public policy but it is being used. This forces the emergency patient to seek care at a different facility.

Many hospitals have been forced to pay physicians to take call so as to get the coverage they needed. Some specialists are paid over $1,000.00 per night just to carry the on-call beeper. This is not even in-house call; it is just to be available by phone and to come in if necessary. Not a bad source of income if you can get it.

Because of EMTALA, all who take call must be aware of their duty to patients with whom they have not yet established a physician-patient relationship. The liabilities associated with EMTALA violations are separate and distinct from those associated with medical malpractice.

"There is no better way of exercising the imagination
than to study the law.
No poet ever interpreted nature
as freely as a lawyer interprets the truth."
~ Jean Girandoux (1882-1944)

"The first duty of society is justice."
~ Alexander Hamilton[89]

Talk #13: The Emergency Medical Treatment and Active Labor Act (EMTALA)

Review, Recall, and Action

Citations

[75] *Millard v. Corrado,* 14 S.W.3d (Mo. App. E.D. 1999).
[76] Id.
[77] Id.
[78] Id.
[79] Restatement (Second) of Torts, section 324A.
[80] *Millard v. Corrado,* 14 S.W.3d (Mo. App. E.D. 1999).
[81] 42 USCA section 1395dd.
[82] EMTALA under subparagraph (B).
[83] 934 F.2d 1362 (5th Cir. 1991).
[84] 42 USCA 1395 cc(a)(1)(I).
[85] www.uplaw.net/faq.htm.
[86] *Roberts v. Galen of Virginia,* 525 U.S. 249 (1999).
[87] These children are born with a significant portion of the brain missing. It is a fatal condition.
[88] *In re Baby K,* 16 F3d 590 (4th Cir. 1994).
[89] Alexander Hamilton, *The Quotable Lawyer* 172 (Tony Lyons ed. 2010).

Summary: A Final Word on Fundamental Issues in Health Care Law: Facts, Fiction, and Future

Taking care of patients can be extremely difficult. The anatomy can vary among individuals as can their responses to medications and stress. Every patient is different. Medical practice is an ongoing learning process and, hopefully, practitioners improve as their experience grows over time.

Becoming a medical doctor requires a tremendous commitment. Years of schooling and post graduate training and then life-long continuing education and peer review are requirements of the profession. Physicians are at the bedside or in the operating room on a daily basis. They take care of patients day and night, on weekends and holidays. Illness can occur at any time and the doctors are there. They don't do health care; they practice medicine and learn to do this better every day. Physicians compose a "learned" profession that brings value to our society.

Unfortunately, the value that society attributes to the medical professions is on the wane. A physician's work entails saving lives, relieving pain and suffering, and providing counsel to patients and their families as they face illness. Through the years, the quality of life for those with chronic diseases has been significantly improved, yet our society no longer recognizes physicians and nurses as the valuable resources they once were.

Our society is marginalizing its physicians. Doctors are being looked upon as a special interest group only intent on making money. Physicians and nurses are now labeled as "providers" and patients are "customers." Federal and State bureaucracies are investigating practitioners for fraud in provision and billing for services. Even our teaching hospitals and medical schools are under the microscope and subject to severe financial penalties if their documentation does not meet legal requirements which are constantly changing and even being enforced in a retroactive fashion.

Today, there is more to practicing medicine than just patient care. In order to make a living, physicians must now document with specificity in order to be paid for their services. Third party payers, using Medicare and Medicaid as their models, are constantly changing the rules in hopes of avoiding payments and improving their own bottom lines. Patient care is not their primary focus.

In order to keep up with the changing rules, practitioners must spend more time documenting the medical records which results in less time taking care of patients at the bedside or in the office. It also leads to increased overhead costs to hire coders and other extenders to meet the bureaucratic requirements associated with being paid for the services they provide. And, not surprisingly, the payments continue to go down as the work load goes up.

There have always been risks for those taking care of patients. Practitioners may become infected with diseases such as HIV, Hepatitis, Tuberculosis, and now, even Ebola. Adding to these medical risks are the legal risks that the practitioner must face. Errors in billing, intentional or not, can result in civil and even criminal charges.

The intent of this book is to provide some basic knowledge of various topics in Health Care Law so that providers can better cope with the legal issues they will be facing on a daily basis. Lack of knowledge of the rules is not an excuse and will not be recognized in a court of law.

The statutes are complex and even some lawyers who make this particular area of health care their specialization do not understand all of the nuances of the precepts. In fact, some courts have come up with some very different interpretations of the laws. If the judges and lawyers are confused, what hope is there for the physicians, nurses, hospital administrators and others who are doing their best to help their patients?

Taking care of patients is a noble profession and I have enjoyed my career immensely. I hope that the medical-legal environment does not discourage future generations from pursuing this career path. I would like to think that my knowledge and experience with both patient care and the law expressed in *Medical Malpractice – A Physician's Guide to Navigating the Minefield of Medical Malpractice Law* and *Fundamental Issues in Health Care Law: Facts for the Health Care*

Professional – A Lecture Series will be helpful to my colleagues as they continue to better treat those entrusted to their care.

As Albert Einstein once said, "Not everything that can be counted counts and not everything that counts can be counted." We should not let the politicians and plaintiff's attorneys keep us from doing what we do best – taking care of patients.

Taking care of patients is a noble profession.

Acknowledgements

With love to my wife, Kathleen, and my daughters, Johanna and Millicent. Their patience, encouragement, and inspiration were invaluable through the years spent in law school, doing research for, and writing this book.

To Victoria Houseman Bromley who edited the first drafts of the book to make the writing understandable to the non-lawyer, and for reorganizing the sequence of chapters to clarify the applicable legal process and associated issues.

To Glen Aubrey and the team at Creative Team Publishing who were willing to take on this project despite the paucity of work in this area and not being sure if the intended audience would even be interested.

To Justin Aubrey for his logo and cover designs.

To Randy Beck for the website design and instructions on marketing to get the existence of this book out to interested parties.

To my parents, whose emphasis on education helped in forming my career; this has not been an easy road.

To Kyle Wiggins and Steve Barlow, fellow law school students who were willing to help the unconventional heart surgeon who was juggling an active surgical practice while trying to meet the academic requirements of the school.

To my medical colleagues who insisted that this work be done to help level the playing field in the process and intricacies of malpractice law.

To professors, residents, nurses, and other health care providers who helped make me a better surgeon through the years.

Products and Services

Products:

Dr. Weiman has authored two books, available through his website: www.MedicalMalpracticeAndTheLaw.com.

1. *Medical Malpractice – A Physician's Guide to Navigating the Minefield of Medical Malpractice Law*
2. *Fundamental Issues in Health Care Law: Facts for the Health Care Professional – A Lecture Series*

Services:

Dr. Weiman has written and offers a timely lecture series that addresses essential topics in Health Care Law. The lecture series contains 13 talks, each designed to effectively communicate the facts a health care professional needs to know.

Each of these talks is contained in *Fundamental Issues in Health Care Law: Facts for the Health Care Professional – A Lecture Series.*

The contents of the book and the Lecture Series are as follows:

- Talk #1: Introduction to Law
- Talk #2: Health Courts
- Talk #3: Stark Reality
- Talk #4: Doctrine of Informed Consent
- Talk #5: Futility
- Talk #6: Resident Personnel Files: Are They Discoverable?
- Talk #7: Themes for Malpractice Defense
- Talk #8: Health Care Talking Points
- Talk #9: Regulation of Provider Conduct: Medicare and Medicaid
- Talk #10: Morbidity and Mortality Conference: What Is Protected? What Is Discoverable?
- Talk #11: The Medical Expert Witness
- Talk #12: The Federal Tort Claims Act and the National Practitioner Data Bank
- Talk #13: The Emergency Medical Treatment and Active Labor Act (EMTALA)

Dr. Weiman has presented as a visiting professor on numerous occasions. You are invited to contact him through his website, to arrange your lecture presentations, and for more information.

www.MedicalMalpracticeAndTheLaw.com

Citations

[1] Rule of construction – also known as a canon of construction; these are "rules used in construing legal instruments, esp. contracts and statutes." Black's Law Dictionary, Seventh Edition.
[2] Richard A. Posner, The Federal Courts: Crisis and Reform 276, (1985). In Black's Law Dictionary, Seventh Edition.
[3] Black's Law Dictionary, Seventh Edition.
[4] For example, *Roe v. Wade,* or *Bush v. Gore.*
[5] Id.
[6] *Marbury v. Madison,* 5 U.S. (1 Cranch) 137 (1803).
[7] "A writ issued by a superior court to compel a lower court or a government officer to perform mandatory or purely ministerial duties correctly. Black's Law Dictionary.
[8] 5 U.S. (1 Cranch) at 177-78.
[9] *Bush v. Gore…..*
[10] Dictum; a statement of opinion or belief held to be authoritative because of the dignity of the person making it. Black's Law Dictionary, Seventh edition, Bryan Garner, editor-in-chief.
[11]Janice Mulligan, Chair of Standing Committee on Medical Professional Liability. 2006.
[12] United States Constitution Article III section 1.
[13] United States Constitution Article V.
[14] Adamy, Janet: Wall Street Journal, Red Flags in Medicare Billing. July 9, 2014.
[15] *US ex rel Baklid-Kunz v. Halifax Medical Center*
[16] *Schloendorff v. Society of New York Hospital,* 105 N.E. 92, 93 (1914)
[17] Id.
[18] *Canterbury v. Spence,* 464 F.2d 772 (D.C. Cir) (1972)
[19] The Supreme Court has stated that this right is evident in the penumbra (shadowed regions) formed by emanations from the Bill of Rights in the 1st, 3rd, 4th, 5th, and 9th amendments)
[20] "Battery" is an unwanted, offensive touching
[21] *Cardwell,* 724 S.W.2d at 749
[22] Idaho Code sec.39-4306
[23]*Kovacs v. Freeman,* 957 S.W.2d 251 (Ky. 1997)

[24] Evidence indicating that the thing to be proved is highly probable or reasonably certain; this is a greater burden than preponderance of the evidence, the standard applied in most civil cases, and less than evidence beyond a reasonable doubt, the norm for criminal trials
[25] In *re Guardianship of Schiavo*, 789 So. 2d 348 (Fla. 2001)
[26] 792 So.2d 551 (Fla. 2d DCA 2001)
[27] The Fourteenth Amendment says in part "…nor shall any State deprive any person of life, liberty, or property, without due process of law…"
[28] *Cruzan v. Director, Missouri Department of Health.*
[29] 285 U.S. 262, 311 (1982)
[30]Tennessee Rules of Evidence, Article 5: Privileges, Rule 501 (1990).
[31] T.C.A. Section 63-6-219(e).
[32] Tennessee Peer Review Law, Tenn. Code Ann. Section 63-219(c) (1967).
[33] *Alexander A. Stratienko, MD, v. Chattanooga-Hamilton County Hospital Authority, et al,* No. E2005-01043-SC-S09-CV-filed May 14, 2007.
[34] *Garza v. Scott and White Memorial Hospital,* 234 F.R.D. 617 (2005).
[35] Texas Health and Safety Code, Section 161.032.
[36] Tennessee Code Annotated, Section 68-11-272. This is now known as the "Tennessee Patient Safety and Quality Improvement Act of 2011." Tennessee Code Annotated, Section 63-1-150 became effective April 8, 2014. This law further protects the Quality Improvement Committee (QIC) by securing record confidentiality.
[37] Tennessee Rules of Evidence Rule 702.
[38]Contiguous states are the states bordering Tennessee. These states are Mississippi, Alabama, Arkansas, Georgia, Kentucky, Missouri, North Carolina, and Virginia.
[39] 118 S.W.3d, 323 (Tenn. 2003).
[40] Ward, Laura: *Foolish Words, The most stupid words ever spoken*, PRC Publishing Limited, New York, 2003,
p. 120.
[41]TCA section 29-26-121.
[42] Good faith means "more probable than not."
[43] A dismissal with prejudice means the plaintiff cannot refile the lawsuit even if he corrects the problem.
[44] Geneva Foundation for Medical Education and Research.
[45] Bernadine Healy, "Behind the Baby Count," US News and World Report, September 24, 2006
[46] The Lasker Award, often a precursor for the Nobel Prize in Medicine, was named after her.

[47] *United States v. Krizek,* 111 F.3d 934 (D.C. Cir. 1997).
[48] *United States v. Pani,* 717 F.Supp 1013 (S.D.N.Y. 1989).
[49] *United States v. Lorenzo,* 768 F.Supp 1127 (E.D. Pa 1991).
[50] *Peterson v. Weinberger,* 508 F.2d 45 (5th Cir. 1975).
[51] *United States v. Krizek,* 111 F.3d 934 (D.C. Cir. 1997).
[52] PATH is the acronym for Physicians At Teaching Hospitals
[53] Ruth SoRelle, Tracking a Tangled PATH, **Circulation,** 1998; 97: 2191.
[54] *Weekoty v. United States,* 30 R.Supp.2d 1343 (D.N.M. 1998).
[55] *Syposs v. United States,* 63 F.Supp.2d 301 (W.D.N.Y. 1999).
[56] Tennessee Rules of Evidence, Rule 401.
[57] Tennessee Rules of Evidence, Rule 407. This rule deals with subsequent remedial measures.
[58] USA Today, October 19, 1998, Section D, 1-2.
[59] New York Times, September 13, 1995, Section B, 3.
[60] Gross negligence is defined as "a conscious, voluntary act or omission in reckless disregard of a legal duty and of the consequences to another party.
[61] "Reckless disregard" means "a conscious indifference to the consequences (of an act)."
[62] *LA CMA Physician,* September 1997, 29-34.
[63] *A Surgeon's Little Instruction Book.*
[64] Prima facie is a legal term meaning that the plaintiff has produced "enough evidence to allow the trier-of-fact to infer the fact at issue and rule in the plaintiff's favor." **Black's Law Dictionary**
[65] John Langbein, 52 U. Chi. L. Rev. 823, 835 (1985).
[66] Lee Mickus, 27 Creighton L. Rev. 773, 787-788 (1994).
[67] Id.
[68] Id.
[69] Id.
[70] *Crumley v. Memorial Hospital,* 509 F. Supp.531, aff'd, 647 F. Supp. 164.
[71] *Rose v. HCA Health* ***Services of*** *Tennessee,* 947 S.W.2d, 144.
[72] *Ralph v. Nagy,* 749 F. Supp. 164.
[73] *United States v. Smith,* 499 U.S. 160, 166 (1991).
[74] VHA Handbook 1100.17.
[75] *Millard v. Corrado,* 14 S.W.3d (Mo. App. E.D. 1999).
[76] Id.
[77] Id.
[78] Id.
[79] Restatement (Second) of Torts, section 324A.
[80] *Millard v. Corrado,* 14 S.W.3d (Mo. App. E.D. 1999).

[81] 42 USCA section 1395dd.
[82] EMTALA under subparagraph (B).
[83] 934 F.2d 1362 (5th Cir. 1991).
[84] 42 USCA 1395 cc(a)(1)(I).
[85] www.uplaw.net/faq.htm.
[86] *Roberts v. Galen of Virginia,* 525 U.S. 249 (1999).
[87] These children are born with a significant portion of the brain missing. It is a fatal condition.
[88] *In re Baby K,* 16 F3d 590 (4th Cir. 1994).
[89] Alexander Hamilton, *The Quotable Lawyer* 172 (Tony Lyons ed. 2010).

Index

A

B

C

D

E

F

G

H

I

J

K

L

M

N

O

P

Q

R

S

T

U

V

W

Y

www.MedicalMalpracticeAndTheLaw.com

CPSIA information can be obtained at www.ICGtesting.com
Printed in the USA
LVOW07s1416160115

423128LV00002B/2/P